CENTENNIAL CELEBRATION OF
STEAMBOAT NAVIGATION ON INLAND WATERS
PITTSBURGH PA. OCT. 31 1911

IMAGES OF AMERICA

A Panorama of History in Photographs

Oh, the dreams of our youth!
How beautiful they are—
And how perishable.
—Samuel Langhorne Clemens

Smithsonian Books, Washington, D.C.

Page 1: Rudolf Eickemeyer, Jr., captured a real life Huck Finn with his photograph of 1901; Pages 2-3: oilmen in Blue Ridge, Texas, strike it rich; Pages 4-5: the Centennial Celebration of Steamboat Navigation on Inland Waterways is held on the Pittsburgh wharf in 1911; Page 6: the strain of the Civil War years appears clearly on the face of Abraham Lincoln in the famous Alexander Gardner photograph taken four days before the president's assassination in 1865; Page 7-8: a woman jumps over a stool in one of Eadweard Muybridge's pioneering studies of movement before the advent of motion pictures.

THE SMITHSONIAN INSTITUTION
Secretary Robert McC. Adams
Assistant Secretary for Public Service Ralph Rinzler
Director, Smithsonian Institution Press Felix C. Lowe
SMITHSONIAN BOOKS
Editor-in-Chief Patricia Gallagher
Administrative Assistant Anne P. Naruta
Senior Editor Alexis Doster III
Editors Joe Goodwin, Amy Donovan, John F. Ross
Research Bryan D. Kennedy
Research Interns Mark G. Lazen, Diana Frankfurter
Acting Senior Picture Editor Frances C. Rowsell
Picture Editor R. Jenny Takacs
Picture Research Carrie E. Bruns, Ann Monroe Jacobs, Anne P. Naruta, Paula Ballo-Dailey
Picture Assistant Sebastian C. Hayman
Copy Editor Tracy Samuel
Production Editor Patricia Upchurch
Production Assistant Martha Sewall
Business Manager Stephen J. Bergstrom
Marketing Director Gail Grella
Marketing Manager Barbara Erlandson
Product Specialist Kate Adams

Library of Congress Cataloging-in-Publication Data
Images of America.

Includes index.
1. United States—History—1865-
—Pictorial works. 2. United States—History—1849-1877—
Pictorial works.
E661.I43 1989   973   89-11322
ISBN 0-89599-023-7 (alk. paper)
Manufactured in the United States of America
First Edition
10 9 8 7 6 5 4 3 2 1

CONTENTS

INTRODUCTION
STOPPING THE WORLD

Photography is a time machine, a truly magnificent vehicle that can whisk us back fifteen decades in a single bound and freeze shining moments in mid-passage. Look into the eyes of patriot David Kinnison, who participated in the Boston Tea Party and the Battle of Lexington, and we can peer almost into the Revolutionary War era. Examine the sly smiles of Butch Cassidy and his gang, and we're back in the Wild West. In a tame and elegant setting we meet a young woman, opposite, whose charm speaks of those special days in San Francisco before the earthquake of 1906. Alas, not even her name has survived.

Thanks largely to curators and archivists of the Smithsonian Institution's vast photographic resource, our particular voyage into the past is as remarkable as the people noted above. Smithsonian experts and their colleagues throughout the country are the masters who create the mirror in which the nation can see and know its heart and soul. They graciously preserve and pass on the stories and views that bring America's lively, gritty, and warmhearted past to life again. We offer our sincere gratitude for their assistance at every step.

Though *Images of America* contains only a few hundred pictures, this work draws its strength from literally millions of private albums, informal collections, home movies, videos, and other personal photographic treasures. Every one of us has family pictures, and they fit—far more neatly than most people realize—into the pictorial resource of American history. To honor the private legacy, our images are not just another gathering of famous pictures from "Great Events." By and large, they reveal people as themselves, engaged in everyday life. Each picture is compelling; each almost jumped out of the collections, beguiling the researchers, and choosing itself from the millions of possibilities. Most of these views are only rarely seen in print and quite a few have never been published before. In terms of quality, the images are usually mint bright, from superbly conserved collections, and seldom tainted with the yellow or orange "sepia color" that, though nostalgic, often shows that a valuable print is sick or dying.

For such reasons, the reader can expect to feel afresh the irresistible influence of people working together to develop an almost virgin land. In fact, the photograph and John Deere's steel plow—the kind that opened up the prairie—both arrived on the American scene in 1839. Change, and the accelerating rate of change since then, have been astounding. And *Images of America* captures these changes through splendid reproduction of the original black-and-white views. For maximum depth and clarity, both black and gray inks are employed on the press, and the reproductions for printing have been prepared with the latest specialized laser technology. This improved medium conveys a remarkable amount of visual information and opens widest our window into the past. To keep the readers' photographic past clear and healthy, a special chapter has been included on basic conservation and safe display methods.

Just a half century into our future—and surely at the Smithsonian—a small editorial group will document the 200th anniversary of photography in America. Today, we operate in the "hands-on" era, thumbing through tons of prints to make our selections. Tomorrow's editors will be aided by electronics and highly sophisticated computers, but, however technologically advanced, they too, will be entirely captivated by America's rich yesteryear. They'll also know a greater thrill because hundreds of thousands of fresh images, many from the early days, will have since come to light.

The editors of Smithsonian Books dedicate the present work to the editors of 2039, who will see even more of the honored past than it has been our privilege to behold.

PART ONE
AN AMERICAN ALBUM

D. Vogt O'Connor

This book celebrates the first century-and-a-half of American photography. It is our national family album, made possible by the nineteenth-century development of photography in both England and France. Jacques Louis Mandé Daguerre of France and William Henry Fox Talbot of England separately announced successful photographic experiments in 1839. Within the year, American artists and scientists were making photographs.

Europeans such as Sir Humphry Davy and Thomas Wedgwood had experimented with making photographs much earlier. And in 1827 the first permanent photograph was made by French amateur scientist Joseph Nicephore Niépce after an eight-hour exposure. Daguerre, a partner of Niépce, became famous when his accidental discovery of a practical photographic process, the daguerreotype, captured the world's attention.

Painter and inventor Samuel F.B. Morse was the first American to actually view a daguerreotype. He wrote glowingly:

> The exquisite minuteness of the delineation cannot be conceived. No painting or engraving ever approached it. . . . The impressions of interior views are Rembrant /sic/ perfected.

Daguerre's English rival, William Henry Fox Talbot, was a scholar of Assyrian cuneiform, an amateur botanist, and an inventor of microscopes and motors. Like Niépce, Talbot was creating photographs before Daguerre (1835). Talbot's calotypes have less detail and a softer appearance than daguerreotypes. The calotypes never became popular in the United States because the process was restricted by patent. The license fee drove the first American patent holders, the Langenheim brothers of Philadelphia, to bankruptcy. The calotype, which produced both a negative and a positive, led to today's photographic processes with which endless prints can be manufactured. Each daguerreotype, like a painting, is unique.

Daguerre's little book of instructions reached the United States during September 1839, and American inventors, tinkerers, and scientists set about translating its 79 pages from the French. D.W. Seager, an Englishman living in New York is credited as first to duplicate the process and make an image (1839). Samuel F. B. Morse, Robert Cornelius, John Draper, Joseph Saxton, and Alexander Wolcott are numbered among the earliest photo pioneers. Little wonder they first made architectural studies, landscapes, and still lifes: exposures took almost forever.

Their human subjects stood painfully still for long periods under bright light to be immortalized by the camera. One sitter's portrait took "eight minutes, with the strong sunlight shining on his face and tears trickling down his checks while . . . the operator promenaded the room with watch in hand, calling out the time every five seconds."

Relatively inexpensive, photography became an appealing democratic medium. It let every man or woman be both subject and creator of images. Each community could document its elder statesmen, its old soldiers, and its *Mayflower* descendants. Americans photographed the things they were most proud of: their families, their inventions, and the western frontier.

In searching for an American equivalent to European images of cathedrals and monuments, American photographers discovered their landscapes. They followed the exploration of the American West through expeditions and the gold rush. Each era of photography was shaped by the predominant concerns of the time.

Early photographers used fine-art conventions to lend distinction to portrait subjects and frontier towns. Through clever placement of props, such as classical columns, American photographers proudly claimed roots in European, and even Greek and Roman, traditions. The use of portraiture to link oneself metaphorically to earlier traditions is as old as Roman portrait sculpture. By incorporating the new with the old, an evolving sense of national identity is recorded in photography.

Preceding pages: Sex goddess of 1902, Evelyn Nesbit appears as a "Tired Butterfly" by Rudolf Eickemeyer, Jr. These pages: A cobbler plies his trade *c.* 1860.

During its first 150 years, the growth of the photographic industry mirrored the expansion of the nation, moving from a cottage craft to a major industry with thousands of products, tens of thousands of employees, and millions of practitioners.

As the nation grew, so did the Smithsonian Institution, from a small study collection, laboratory, and library to the world's largest museum complex. Early Smithsonian scientists made and collected photographs to document expeditions, field work, research, discoveries, collections, and staff.

As early as 1859, the first Smithsonian secretary, Joseph Henry, suggested using photography to record a visiting American Indian delegation. In 1888 Samuel F. B. Morse's historic photographic apparatus was bought by Thomas Smillie, first curator of photography. In 1896 Smillie bought fifty photographs, the first documented purchase of photographs as art by a major museum. Collections grew rapidly.

During 1984, five years before photography's sesquicentennial, the Smithsonian Archives began to survey and describe these collections for a multi-volume *Guide to Photographic Collections at the Smithsonian Institution*. Working like archeologists, the staff went to every office, attic, and basement in the Museum complex. Sealed boxes were opened. Curators were interviewed. There were exciting results. The Archives staff discovered some of the world's oldest, largest, and most varied photographic collections. Before the survey project is completed, project staff anticipate describing more than ten million photographs.

These three hundred images are only a tiny portion of the eight million photographs surveyed so far. The *Guide* series shows many hundreds more. They are hors d'oeuvres to whet the appetites of photographic scholars, historians, and the public. The photographs have tremendous potential for future research, publications, and exhibitions.

Many pages in the American album are blank. Photographs are a fragile heritage prone to destruction by neglect. Every day, though, significant images are discovered tucked away in basements and attics around the country. The images document our cultural heritage, our landscapes, and our human endeavors with a poignant immediacy that was first seen in 1839 with the daguerreotype. The sesquicentennial of American photography is a reminder of the wealth of images not yet preserved. If the American family album is ever to reflect the full richness of our social diversity, it must be done now before the fragile legacy of our pioneering photographers has vanished.

SILVER MEN AND PLATINUM WOMEN

Smithsonian's earliest photo portrait, of Henry Fitz, Jr., probably dates from January 1840. Top, Thomas Eakins poses with his sister, Frances, c. 1850.

We met the photographer in the 1840s, we early Americans. He often followed the snake-oil medicine man into town. He'd pull up at the stagecoach stop, or roll his wagon, rattling with copper plates and bottles of chemicals, onto the riverboat landing and slosh ashore to drum up trade. He set up shop all over our young, bucolic United States, and lured us in: "Come one, come all! Visit the Professor's Daguerrean Saloon and find immortality!"

And we came. Leaving our likenesses to our descendants appealed to us, especially since a visit to the "professor" was less expensive than a session before the easel of Mr. Thomas Sully or Mr. Samuel F.B. Morse, or even one of the lesser known itinerant portraitists.

Daguerreotypes and photographs cost us less in money but more in pain. The professor often turned out to be a tyrant who crammed us into some fake parlor setting where we suffered, awkwardly positioned, unable to move for whole minutes at a time. He seemed never satisfied with what he saw when he ducked behind his mysterious mahogany-and-brass box, perched on its cumbrous tripod, and peered into whatever was hidden under that ubiquitous black cloth. Women and presidents he treated with impatient courtesy. The rest of us he bent to his will like a top sergeant—barely civil to honest folk who tried to cooperate, snarling impatiently at children who couldn't help but twitch and writhe in their discomfort.

When the ordeal was finally over and the chemical wizardry wrought with mercury or salts of silver, platinum, or even palladium, we had our portraits. Generally we looked a little funereal. After all, we'd been staring stone-still at the lens for about a minute, and our eyes were glazed or tearful for want of a blink, our mouths strained shut to forestall a cough, a sneeze, even a rebellious hoot of laughter. You of the future were vouchsafed an image of sorts. But judging from it, you might never guess that we were a people who probably laughed more than you do.

We ourselves were seldom delighted with the results. They say Ralph Waldo Emerson hated his daguerreotype. Sojourner Truth, one of our earliest battlers for the rights of blacks and women, considered her photograph a mere shadow and sold copies of it to—in her words—"support the Substance." And Abraham Lincoln, subjected to many studio sittings, could only consider a likeness "horridly" true.

But the effort and agony that produced our first photographs have given you modern Americans a magical glimpse of our lives. You may regard history as a dreary compilation of dates and names, gray words on white pages. But we of the past really lived. We really thought and acted. We have a good story to tell.

We were much the same sort of people as you—and yet not quite. Remember your great aunt? The words she used? The songs she sang? The tales she told about *her* great aunt? She gave you a window to the past. So too does a box of faded letters in your attic. Skim over the dated formalities and you'll find universal feelings, still as fresh as they were when we wrote them.

Our old photographs probably give you the best touchstone of all. Here are true visions of America when square-riggers crowded our waterfronts, when our streets were either mud, dust, or slush, when distant mountains rose crystal-clear, barely touched by man.

History dull? Look at us carefully! Here are the clothes we wore—long dress and ribboned bonnet, pinafore, broadcloth suit and bow tie. Here are small episodes of adventure, play, joy, sadness, all familiar to you today. Here are hands and faces lined by hardships perhaps more basic than any you know.

And here are eyes that have looked upon bravery and cowardice, honesty and deceit, heroes and villains. Look deeply into our eyes and you may read our pride in this new land we are building. Also our hope for you, our future.

Edwards Park

Patriot Memories

Born in 1736, David Kinnison took part in the Boston Tea Party and opposed the Redcoats at Lexington and Bunker

Hill. At age 111 he sat for his portrait, top. Peter Stephen Du Ponceau, below left, came to America from France as aide-de-camp and secretary to Major General the Baron von Steuben and saw active service during the Revolution. Albert Gallatin, above, emigrated to America from Switzerland in 1780. He served as Thomas Jefferson's treasury secretary and negotiated an end to the War of 1812.

A Kind of Earthly Immortality

Regal in her ruffled bonnet, opposite, an unidentified matriarch mirrors the lively spirit of young America. Top, famed for his portrait studios and Civil War photos, Mathew Brady stands beside Juliette Handy Brady and Mrs. Haggerty, *c.* 1850. Stage props, neck rests, and chemical magic await clients at an old-time studio.

22

Capt. Atlee Putnam, opposite, displays his warlike splendor on a carte-de-visite produced by Brady in Washington, D.C. Friends and associates began exchanging such mementoes after 1854, when a French process facilitated the production of multiple prints. Bashful maiden is immortalized in one of America's earliest outdoor portraits, left. She was discovered in the notebooks of Titian Ramsay Peale, scientist, explorer, patent examiner, and a photographic experimenter of Washington, D.C.

Arctic whalers of the 1880s, posing in New Bedford, Massachusetts, wear fur suits of Inuit (Eskimo) origin. Many early seafarers, traders, and mountain men maintained harmonious relations with North America's traditional peoples. But conflict was common and settlement well under way by 1839, when the camera reached America. Indian power on the Northern Plains had effectively been broken by the 1880s when David F. Barry made his stirring studies of Gall, chief of the Hunkpapa Sioux, opposite. Below, peaceable but of fierce aspect, Inuit of the Bering Strait greet Smithsonian explorer Edward W. Nelson during the 1870s.

African odyssey, the whole tragic episode of Black slavery in the United States, began with the arrival of a few house servants in colonial Virginia. The "Caribbean system," of Portuguese origin, soon promoted mass enslavement of Africans and their transport to America for turning cash crops. Renty, a Congo-born Black, was one of several slaves brought before the camera at a South Carolina plantation during 1850 as part of an anthropological study. By 1890 a New Yorker, Rudolf Eickemeyer, Jr., visited Mt. Meigs, Alabama, to record rural scenes in Dixie after the Civil War, top and opposite.

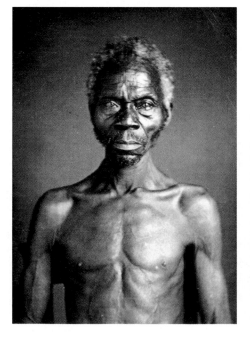

Photos Bring Life Stories to Light

Children born a generation apart meet as adults, *c.* 1908. Mark Twain in his seventies encounters Helen Keller in her late twenties. Though blind, deaf, and mute from an early age, Miss Keller overcame her handicaps. A dynamic person, she traveled to meet the great figures of her day. To "see" Twain, she touched his features. To "hear" him talk, she placed her hands near his vocal cords. Twain, born Samuel Clemens, sat for a daguerreotype at age 15. Recently orphaned, he apprenticed himself to the printer of the Hannibal, Missouri, newspaper. The name "Sam" shows in

big metal type, but young Clemens placed the letters backward because he knew that the daguerre process made "flopped" images. To see what the original "Tom Sawyer" looked like, view Sam's picture in a mirror. Helen Keller, at far left, appears as a child with Anne Sullivan, her teacher and friend.

Ahead of Their Time

Hand on hip or arms folded, the woman of the late 1800s often had a mind of her own and certainly ruled the domestic roost—at least kitchen and nursery. The resolute females pictured here, though, stand out from the Victorian crowd. Opposite, headstrong daughter of Theodore, "Princess" Alice Roosevelt earns her reputation. She is noted for her beauty, strong will and sharp tongue. The other three women are part of America's mildly Bohemian art scene. Top, in Philadelphia during 1897, Jennie Kershaw poses for artist Thomas Eakins. (Please see page 17.) Miss Kershaw was employed at the Moore College of Art, a famous professional school for women. Caroline and Anita Vedder, left, are wife and daughter of artist Elihu Vedder who, after the Civil War, worked as an illustrator of fantastic tales.

Art World

Henry Wadsworth Longfellow and his daughter pose in an 1860s drawing room, right. An artist ruled squares onto the print to guide him in copying the figures onto an oil painting, one showing the two Americans beneath a grand Roman arch. Also employing the camera as a visual notetaker, artist Thomas Eakins made the nude study of an unidentified model in a classical setting and pose, below. Opposite, famed society painter John Singer Sargent works in his Paris studio during 1885; behind him, the "Portrait of Madame X," a work that ruffled critics during its 1884 debut. They saw it as eccentric and erotic. A scandal ensued.

Scientist in Motion

While artists valued photos, some scorned the camera as a mechanical *idiot savant*—yielding views too candid, far too clinical for the delicate public sensibilities of the day. Scientists, though, reveled in the literal lens, especially as it gained speed and was thus able to freeze time and motion. Thomas Eakins experimented with multiple exposures on one film plate. With a battery of cameras controlled by clockwork, Eadweard Muybridge pioneered in the area of sequential views: here his 1887 self-portrait in 44 frames. Earlier, one of his photo sequences proved that a race horse can lift all four hoofs from the ground at the same time. Motion pictures lay just around the corner.

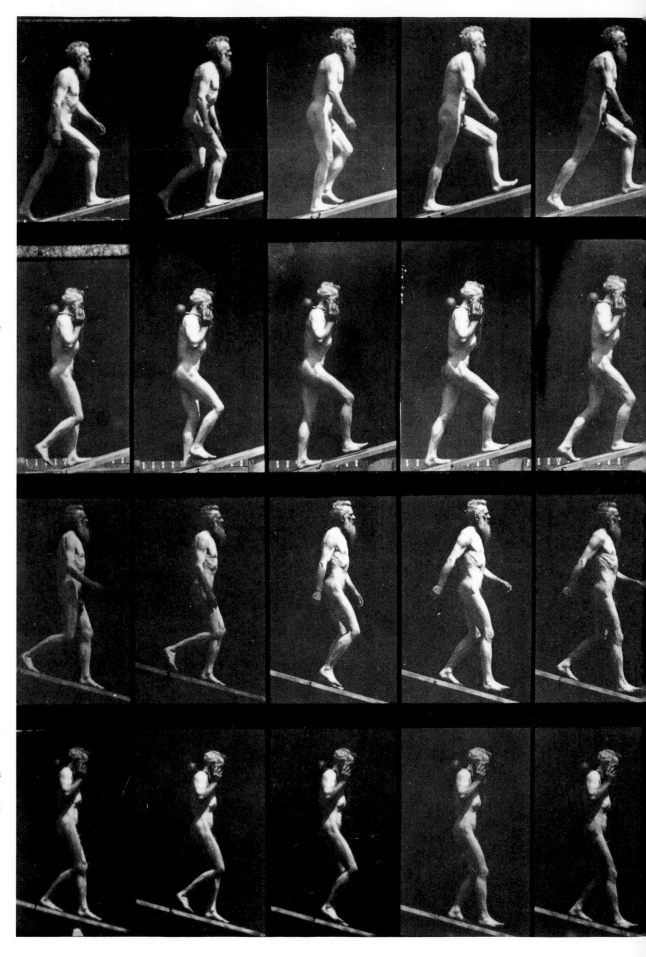

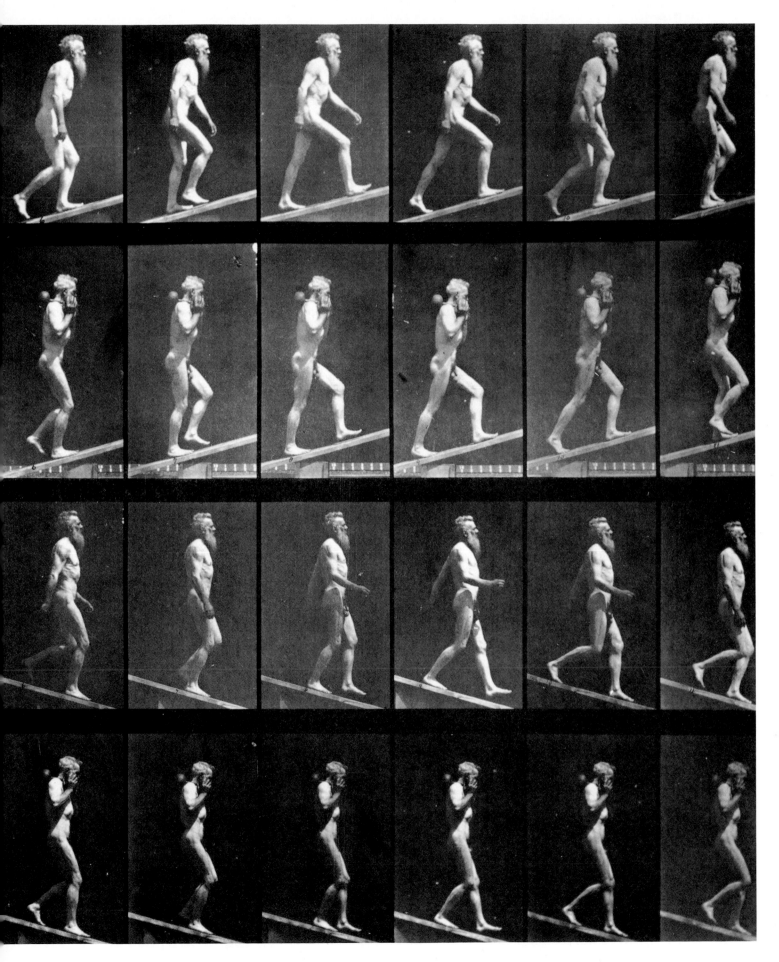

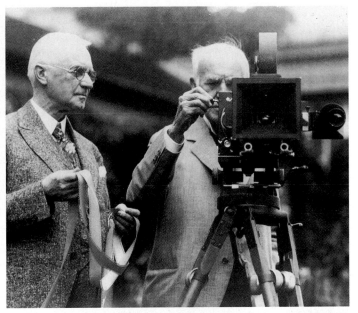

Masters of the Magic Lantern

At top, snapshot pioneer and innovative genius George Eastman works with Thomas Edison—the "Wizard of Menlo Park"—who cranks one of Eastman's multi-shot still cameras. This meeting led to Edison's own cine-industry after 1889. By 1927, silent films gained a voice and sparked an entertainment revolution. The "flickers" and "talkies" depended on dynamos, miles of wire, and operators who regulated the flow of what modern society came to call its "juice," as at left. Keeper of the switches, above, is Ernest McElroy of the Rodney Hunt Machine Company in Orange, Massachusetts, *c.* 1910.

"Love at First Sight"

Still or in motion, photogenic faces captured the heart of the American public during the early decades of the 20th century. Such innocent sex appeal helped sell the stars, as with Nickolas Muray's 1930 fashion photograph of Loretta Young and her pretty sisters, right (Loretta on the left). Thomas S. Hart, from 1917, was a real cowboy who became Hollywood's first great celluloid gunslinger, above. Opposite, "Miss Archer," a 1903 vision by Rudolf Eickemeyer, Jr., helped publicize the New Woman, a durable ideal. Glamour marches on, still an advertising staple.

First in the Class

Charles Spencer Chaplin captured not only the nation's heart but the world's with his most famous character. Here, in a look-alike contest, a troupe of amateur tramps emulates the master, above in mufti, from a 1924 portrait by Nickolas Muray.

A tramp, a gentleman, a poet, a dreamer, a lonely fellow, always hopeful of romance and adventure. — Charles Chaplin (*His own view of the "Little Tramp"*)

HOW WE LIKE TO SEE OURSELVES

"Oh wad some power the giftie gie us to see oursels as others see us!" That wonderful quote from Robert Burns touches a deep chord in us all. Photography gave us such a power. Who among us, when shown images that include oneself, does not immediately zero in on the portion of the picture that we inhabit? Of course, we also have a great affinity for pictures of spouses, children, relatives, and ancestors; perhaps we hope to see a bit of ourselves embodied in them, or vice versa. Certainly one of the solid delights we gain from old family photograph albums is the evidence they provide that one's ancestors were real people who lived out the basic pattern of life much the way we do now. Here's Dad, in the navy during World War II—look how thin he was. And here he is with Mom right before they were married. They were younger then than I am now, and can they really be hugging in front of the camera!

Perhaps there are earlier generations in the album, too. Why does it seem that the older the picture, the more solemn the person? It is useful to recall that the early commercial portrait photographs required very long exposures. Who can hold a smile or any other spontaneous expression for a minute? (Try it and see!) The camera was definitely slower than the eye. We know, for instance, that Lincoln's face was wonderfully animated, but his photos provide little evidence of it. Look at the title page of this book for a portrait from his last studio appointment: a tear runs from his eye from holding back a blink. We do, though, see the beginning of a tired smile. The camera seems to have speeded up to catch just a bit more of his humanity.

But improvements were definitely in the works. With the introduction in the late 1870s of glass-plate negatives that could be coated with chemicals far in advance of the actual exposure and could also be held for processing and printing at a convenient time, non-studio photography became common. Suddenly American photography was boundless.

As we "read" such images, we should remember that the photographic art was dominated by professionals or the most dedicated amateurs up to a century ago. In 1888, though, George Eastman introduced the Kodak camera with flexible film negatives, so easy to use that Eastman could boast, "You push the button, we'll do the rest." Eastman's invention made photography truly democratic—pictures by, for, and of the people.

In browsing through the great American album of photographs we become aware not only of the key figures and events of history but of the richly detailed evidence of everyday America. Beyond all the thrilling and famous events we discover the essence of the activities of the American people. That's our real identity: that's how we like to see ourselves in our own albums.

Ulysses S. Grant and his family endure a long, show portrait sitting in 1883. Seven years later George Eastman clicks his quick Kodak, top.

Mary M. Ison

Pillars of the Community

In 1905, on a sleepy afternoon in South Boston, Virginia, the town's menfolk gather. Store owners Ed Cage and W. Cabel Waller grasp the porch pillars; other notables include Mr. Ebley, the town telegraph operator (atop the barrel), and a uniformed policeman. Many such stores had a liars' bench (in the background, at right), which promoted business and the telling of tall tales. Dr. William Brann, shown above with his family in 1933, delivered more than 5,000 babies in South Boston and the surrounding Virginia countryside.

Caught on film, but perhaps never in life, the Wild Bunch, opposite, included Robert LeRoy Parker, better known as Butch Cassidy (seated farthest right) and Harry Longbaugh, the Sundance Kid (seated farthest left). The fate of these two desperate characters is not certain; they may have died in Bolivia in 1909, or lived to old age at home. Callousness and brashness shine from the eyes of 33-year-old Jesse James, left, whose feats of murder, robbery, and plundering came to typify the dangers of the American West. His 16 years as an outlaw ended in 1887 when a former gang member shot him in the back of the head. A young George Armstrong Custer, top, poses at West Point where he was a cadet. Although Custer graduated at the very bottom of his class in 1861, he quickly proved his prowess during the Civil War, becoming the youngest Union general—and one of the best.

Men Perspire, Ladies Glow All Summer

Summertime brought sunny days and vacation memories worth preserving on film. In the Gilded Age, society photographer Rudolf Eickemeyer, Jr., captured the ideal of the lazy-hazy season, above. This image of Miss Mary McConnell, however, was taken in his New York studio. Though its name and location have eluded scholars, the camp, opposite, welcomed summer folks around 1890. Its ambience, at least, is well realized through nine sylvan views. They survived together and intact because of their decorative fabric backing. Comfortable camps like the one opposite often sprang up in the mountains stretching from Maine to Georgia along the Atlantic Seaboard. Thus began the era of that agonizing question for vacationers of the increasingly prosperous middle class, "Dear, shall we go to the mountains or the seashore this year?"

On its maiden voyage across the North Atlantic in April 1912, the unthinkable happened to the unsinkable. The *Titanic* hit an iceberg and went to the bottom of the sea. Only one-third of the more than 2,000 passengers were rescued, most of those by the passing Cunard liner *Carpathia*. On board the *Carpathia*, teenager Bernice Palmer snapped the image of two unidentified women, opposite, probably rescued from the *Titanic*. She also photographed a group of women and a child dressed in ill-fitting clothes, top. *Carpathia* passengers took the survivors to their hearts, supplying warm coats and beds. Above, young honeymooners from Brooklyn, New York, console Mrs. Charles Hayes who lost her husband in the disaster.

Hey! Look At Me

American bathing beauties during the 1920s display inches of bare legs and miles of wide smiles, left. Daring American bathing styles soon appeared on British and European beaches. At the turn of the century, American women learned much about current fashions by studying fashion plates, such as the early advertisement for a scale company, above. American women also knew how to clown: top, two girls in ladylike bonnets lallygag with doughnuts.

Documenting the nation's romance with the road, Americans took their cameras along on family drives and vacations. Left, tourists tunnel through a sequoia in California during the duster-and-goggles era of the early twentieth century. Note the right-hand drive. Most driver's education consisted of tours around back pastures until the Briscoe Motor Car Company introduced a special model with dual steering, top, in 1917. During the same decade, time management studies by Frank and Lillian Gilbreth saved the American auto industry money (page 122). Later, the Gilbreths became a household name after their daughter wrote the immensely popular *Cheaper By the Dozen*. Above, the Gilbreth family before it had swelled to 12.

Out For a Little Spin

In the 1880s and '90s, cycling became the most popular sport in the nation. More than 10 million people learned to ride in this first wave of bicycle-mania. Enthusiasts formed the League of American Wheelmen and lobbied to exclude professionals hired by bicycle manufacturers from competing in amateur races. League membership soon grew past 100,000. Wires attaching their "ordinaries" to nearby porches bring Boston league members, left, to a standstill, providing the photographer with a few precious seconds in which to capture the group on film.

Let the good times roll.
—Traditional

PART TWO
AMERICA SEEKS ITS DESTINY

Will Stapp

A photograph is so palpably derived from the real world that the photographic image is often confused and identified with its subject: experiencing a photograph becomes a surrogate for experiencing the subject in real life. Looking at a photo of the aged Walt Whitman still brings the viewer a sense of stepping into the room with the poet, opposite. Particularly in the early days of the art, the veracity of the photographic image was unquestioned, and it became a proxy for what it represented.

This distinctive, specific quality of the photographic image had a powerful psychological impact in the nineteenth century that was undoubtedly reinforced by the remarkable dramatic visual properties of the first photographic process adopted in this country, the daguerreotype. Made of a sheet of silver-plated copper, the physical object resembles a mirror, and its image has the same illusion of a tangible, physical presence as a mirror's—except that it reflects back the likeness of someone else or some other thing! To look at a daguerreotype of, say, Daniel Webster, is not merely to learn his appearance; it is to encounter him directly, intimately, and viscerally. This is a powerful and compelling experience today, but to the nineteenth-century person, for whom Webster was a contemporary figure of mythic stature, the experience was intense, highly personal, and virtually religious. It was perhaps less awesome if the image were of a loved one, but the effect was no less emotional and no less genuine.

Especially in the national context, the daguerreotype negated absence and distance and made great persons

59

equally accessible to everyone. This was understood and articulated by critics in the period, and it was consciously exploited by the photographic studios, which—from the very beginning—collected and exhibited the likenesses of the notable men and women of the day. The portraits were displayed to attract customers, who contemplated and were enlightened by their heroes' visages—and could be photographed in the same place, in the same pose, with the same props, by the same photographer.

By 1860, photography was barely twenty years old as a technology and as a medium. Within those two decades, it had not only been quickly transformed from what was essentially a scientific novelty with few real applications into a practical, profitable system for making pictures; but it had also rapidly become an established profession within the United States. Moreover, that profession and the images it created had almost immediately assumed important, dynamic functions in American life. Beginning with the opening of the first studios in early 1840, the camera became a particularly effective instrument of social integration and nationalism, primarily because of the personal and public portraits that were its chief product at that time. And the galleries themselves (or at least the major ones) came to be a vital, albeit temporary, force in American cultural life through the portraits they displayed. In an era of expansionism and migration, personal images—pictures of loved ones—symbolically and emotionally united families that were physically dispersed across this growing nation. Public images—portraits of the men (and some women) in public life who were then considered to be the living embodiments of the nation's distinctive spirit and character—were morally uplifting, and inspired national pride. They imparted a sense of personal identification with the country's leadership and hence with the country itself.

Even though today we take them more for granted because they are more familiar, personal images still serve the same purpose now as they did then. But because the role of the public image has altered substantially in the intervening years, it is important to consider the unprecedented impact the photographic image had in the mid-nineteenth century. Before photography all systems for making images were manual and therefore inherently limited by the skill of the artist. No matter how accomplished the draftsman, the veracity of the image was suspect because human agency was directly involved. The photographic image, however, was

Preceding pages: Walt Whitman, aging poet, reposes c. 1891, (from T. Eakins). These pages: Civil War soldier (8th Pennsylvania Reserve) displays a tattered flag.

generated by the chemical action of light working in a machine. As a consequence, the nineteenth century automatically presumed a photograph to be utterly infallible in its accuracy.

In the mid-1850s a new technology, the so-called wet collodion or wet-plate process, began to replace the daguerreotype in America, and by 1860 had made it virtually obsolete. While it was no less tedious to prepare a wet-plate than a daguerreotype, the new process produced a negative from which an almost limitless number of prints could be made. This did not substantially affect the demand for or use of private portraits (although it made them more convenient to keep, mail, display, or store), but it had substantial impact on public portraiture—and subsequently on the studios—because it made public likenesses distributable on a mass-production basis while it also reduced their unit cost and made them more affordable. One immediate consequence of this was that photographs printed from collodion negatives played a role in the 1860 presidential campaign that daguerreotypes could not have played in 1856. They unquestionably contributed to the election of Abraham Lincoln.

The Civil War soon followed Lincoln's election. The conflict was as pivotal an event in American photography as it was in American history. The following chapter evokes that decisive struggle. As we have seen, before the Civil War the camera's place had been in the studio; but after 1865 the broad spectrum of the American experience was increasingly seen and recorded by the camera. Photographs documented the exploration of the West, its conquest by the military, and its settlement by pioneers. Photographs recorded the growth of our cities and our industry, and in time their pictures came to be used as powerful weapons by reformers combatting slumlords, sweatshops, and the evils of child labor. All of this was conceptually enabled by the photography of the Civil War and increasingly facilitated by improving photographic technology.

Through photography we have acquired a more vivid and intimate vision of the last 150 years of our nation's life than was ever possible before 1839. But—like any other historical document—these images of our past require careful examination, consideration, and informed interpretation to extract their literal meanings. They are innately ambiguous documents and do not necessarily depict what seems self-evident. Even so, photographs link us directly to our past by making it tangible. In doing so they speak directly to our hearts, and thus have a power and a significance that make them a precious element of our heritage.

61

LINCOLN—
A SINGULAR VISION

Abraham Lincoln in the Civil War years was a compelling subject for a camera, and photography came of age just in time to capture him for his contemporaries and for history. The telegraph, with its instantaneous dissemination of news, combined with photography to make Lincoln, in a sense, the first "media president" and to give the world a unique account of America in that tumultuous period.

When the war began, Mathew Brady, the country's preeminent photographer, resolved to compile a photographic history of it. He and other photographers, accompanied by their so-called "whatizzit wagons"—odd-looking conveyances that carried their equipment and served as their dark rooms—soon became familiar adjuncts to every important military movement. Brady himself employed 20 photographers, later saying he had men "in all parts of the army like a rich newspaper."

In addition to battlefield photographs, the photographers took pictures of nearly every prominent figure of the day, military and civilian. Mary Lincoln was a will-

ing but critical client of Brady's, and the Confederate spies Rose Greenhow and Belle Boyd were reluctant ones. General Ulysses S. Grant found that a photographer's studio could be almost as hazardous as a battlefield. On a Washington visit during March 1864, Grant agreed to pose for his photograph. One of Brady's assistants slipped while adjusting the lighting overhead, and both feet went through the skylight, raining shards of two-inch-thick glass down around the new general-in-chief of the Union armies. Fortunately, none of the pieces hit him, but everyone in the studio waited in fear and dread of his reaction. Grant merely glanced up to see what had happened, and then nonchalantly resumed looking into the camera.

Lincoln was first photographed by Brady in the latter's New York studio on February 27, 1860, the day he addressed the Young Republican Men's Club at Cooper Union. Impressed by the height of the "prairie lawyer" who was gaining national recognition for his debates on the slavery issue, Brady decided to photograph him in a standing pose. Observing Lincoln's long, thin neck and prominent Adam's apple, he asked if he might adjust his collar. "Ah," replied Lincoln, pulling the collar up, "I see you want to shorten my neck."

Lincoln's five-dollar bill portrait, opposite. President of the Confederacy Jefferson Davis and his wife, Varina, above.

"That's just it," Brady admitted, and they both laughed. Lincoln would later say that Brady's photograph and his Cooper Union speech made him president.

On February 23, 1861, the day he arrived in Washington as president-elect amid rumors of war and threats of assassination, and despite the tension all about him, Lincoln went to Brady's studio on Pennsylvania Avenue for his first official picture. He would subsequently be photographed in various settings throughout the war: in the studio, at the White House, at the Capitol, and in the field when he visited army headquarters. Modestly, Lincoln thought the camera "painfully truthful," but he was not unwilling to pose.

While the camera was always candid, photographers were not above a bit of sham. When Brady could not obtain pictures of Confederate generals, he used photographs from an earlier date and had uniforms painted over their civilian clothes.

Because of the involved process and the exposure time required for a photograph, few pictures were taken of an actual battle. On one occasion a photographer persuaded a Union artillery crew to pose as if they were in the act of firing, only to have shells rained on them by Confederates across the way who had been viewing the procedure through field glasses and thought it the real thing. Even scenes taken after a battle were sometimes staged. As the war continued, photographers became inured to the carnage of battle, and for better lighting or more dramatic effect were known to rearrange the bodies before taking the picture.

The impact of a photograph was starkly demonstrated when pictures were released of Union soldiers freed from the Confederate military prison at Andersonville, Georgia, at the end of the war. Photographs of their starving, skeleton-like bodies aroused public wrath and were instrumental in bringing about the trial and execution of the prison commandant.

No photographs, however, caught the tragedy of that time more hauntingly than those taken after Lincoln's assassination, showing Ford's Theatre draped in black crepe, the funeral procession, and the train carrying his body home to Springfield.

Gerry Van der Heuvel

Former slave Gilbert Hunt, left, gained his freedom in 1811 by valiantly rescuing several women and children from a burning Richmond theater. This selfless act won for Hunt the highest status a black man could earn in the antebellum South. For all Americans but especially for Blacks, the Civil War brought social and economic upheaval of a magnitude never seen before or since in this nation. Opposite, after the victory a woman visits a former slave pen in Alexandria, Virginia.

"We'll show the dastard minions what southern pluck can do . . ."

Amid the buildings of Fredericksburg, Virginia, Confederate soldiers, opposite, pose for a photograph on the ruins of a bridge that once spanned the Rappahannock River. While Mathew Brady set up his camera, the cocky men taunted the Northern photographer by yelling, "Before you get to Richmond you have a 'longstreet' to travel, a big 'hill' to climb, and a 'stonewall' to get over." Such boasting referred to the South's outstanding military leaders, who included James Longstreet, Ambrose Hill, and, pictured at left, Thomas "Stonewall" Jackson. Below left, several Confederate pickets warm themselves over a small fire outside of Fredericksburg, where a fierce battle in December 1862 stymied the Union's march on Richmond.

A Northern Avalanche of Soldiers and Supplies

A plenitude of military supplies piles up along a mile of wharves at General Ulysses Grant's City Point, Virginia, supply depot on the James River, opposite. The stockpile elicited the dispirited remark from one Southern clergyman that the Union had "not merely profusion but extravagance." From its well-equipped Union troops drilling near Washington, top, to its artillery batteries on the field at Fredericksburg, above, the North enjoyed superior military striking power and industrial muscle. The North had foundries, powder mills, railroad steam engine factories, textile industries, and rubber plants. Union furnaces roared, producing a formidable threat to Southern hopes for a victory.

Bastion on the Potomac

Daily, the streets of Washington, D.C., revealed the evidences of civil war. From the young drummer boys, opposite, to the infantry musician, right, and the cavalry units at the U.S. Capitol, above, men and boys alike met the call to arms, polishing their brass, practicing their songs, forming their lines in drill, and preparing for the glorious struggle. But Washington also witnessed the realities of war. The president himself grimly sat at a White House window in late July of 1861 and watched exhausted Union troops limp back into town, men slumped in saddles, lying on boards, and covered with crude bandages.

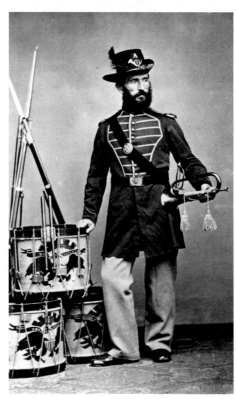

Covered Wagons in War

Union supply wagons crowd the muddy streets of Confederate winter quarters at Centreville, Virginia, above. Only days earlier, the entire rebel force had packed up and moved. Logistics of troop movement and resupply encouraged the exploitation and development of new technological advances, such as telegraphy and photography. From the

Army of the Potomac's Field Telegraph Battery, opposite, messages flashed from far-distant battlefields to headquarters, ushering in a new era of wartime communications. Traveling photographic darkrooms similar to Alexander Gardner's wagon, opposite above—a veritable forerunner of modern newsreel trucks—enabled photographers to help in surveillance work, assist professional mapmakers, and document the

course of events. While supply wagons provided support for tactical combat operations, the Union Army's strategic plans depended on secure rail and water transport. Thousands of cavalry horses, for instance, were carried by train as close to the fighting as possible.

According to photographer Alexander Gardner, this view of Antietam, above right, was taken during the first day of the fearful battle. If so, and scholars think Gardner may have stretched the truth, it is one of the very rare action photographs taken during the Civil War. At Antietam, photographer Mathew Brady drew his cumbersome gear so close to the battle that blasting shells sprayed his equipment with dirt. Never before had

the marks of combat—the destruction and drama, the pathos and irony, the profound moments of history—been captured, made so visible for posterity. The unforgettable figure of Abraham Lincoln, above left, towers over his generals and other officers at General George McClellan's headquarters at Antietam, October 1862. Top, captured southern officer James Washington (left) shares war experiences with friend and

fellow West Point classmate George
Armstrong Custer, a Union officer.

"A sea of anguish"

The technology of warfare far outpaced the science of medicine, and for the wounded soldiers in the Virginia field hospital, left, and others, a bone saw and a shot of brandy bring little solace. For doctors such as the half-dozen army surgeons serving the Union troops in Petersburg, Virginia, top, and the war's only female physician, Mary Walker, above, the conditions were hideous, the tasks daunting. Modern weaponry ripped, tore, and smashed human bodies with extraordinary efficiency. And exposure, infection, and disease proved equally lethal.

Atlanta

Some of the city, such as the mill and the Chattanooga railroad cars, opposite, were destroyed by fleeing Confederate soldiers. A demolished bank stands next to an intact saloon, above. Top, panorama of a residential area. The fall of Atlanta in 1864 crushed southern hopes. As it is today, the city was Dixie's center of commerce and transport.

Eight inches of iron protect the turret of the Union monitor *Passaic,* left, dented by Confederate shells. During the Civil War both sides feverishly experimented with ironclad designs, resulting in developments that presaged the modern American navy. The original Union monitor utilized more than 40 patentable inventions. While approaching two Union ironclads near Savannah, Georgia, the Confederate ram *Atlanta,* above, ran aground, and the monitor *Weehawken* easily battered it into submission with its 11- and 15-inch Dahlgren guns. A sign of the old-fashioned navy was the powder monkey, top, a nimble child who carried bags of gunpowder between a ship's magazines and the guns.

"From these honored dead we take increased devotion. . . ."

Gettysburg, Pennsylvania, November 19, 1863. Town officials, other government dignitaries, and towns-people join a Union regiment, left, as it marches to Cemetery Ridge, site of a ceremony to honor those who fell four months earlier in the war's bloodiest battle. One image of the site of the historic "Gettysburg Address" exists, top. Enlargements from the same photograph, above right and left, reveal Lincoln engulfed by the crowd.

Less than two weeks after General Robert E. Lee surrendered at Appomattox Court House, the flag-draped funeral train bearing Lincoln's body, top, rolled slowly out of Washington on its way to Illinois. Crazed ex-Confederate soldier and conspirator Lewis Paine, opposite, glowers from his cell in Washington Penitentiary shortly before his execution. He had attempted to kill the secretary of state, William Seward, in his bedchamber. Paine and three other conspirators were hanged in the jail yard on July 7, 1865. (Their leader, John Wilkes Booth, had perished in a blazing Maryland farmhouse.) Left, their swinging bodies blur in a Mathew Brady photograph.

Past is Prelude

By the spring of 1865, Richmond, the capital of the Confederacy, lay in ruins, its bridges, factories, mills and arsenals torched by fleeing Confederates. "One mighty pandemonium of war," recalled a rebel gunner as high winds whipped up a fire storm. After visiting Richmond, Lincoln told a gathering on the White House lawn that the fall of the Confederacy was a time to be glad in heart. But from Lincoln the crowd received no patriotic oration, no declarations about heroic deeds and grand causes.

. . . let us bind up the nation's wounds . . . to do all which may achieve and cherish a just and lasting peace. . . .
—Abraham Lincoln

MOVING ON WEST

Top, first rail crossing of the Alleghenies, in 1853, is re-enacted in 1863. During 1889, a grizzled prospector poses on a Colorado peak for William Henry Jackson — "Mustang Jack" — a great explorer-photographer.

Moving West! To many Americans the spirit of the United States is encapsulated in this image. Unlike most of the other nations of the world, the United States is a nation always in the process of creation, developing, growing. Even in the 1980s it is the most dynamic of all nations, recreating itself, reconstructing itself, rebuilding itself with a speed that astonishes the rest of the world.

It is not purely fortuitous that the most famous historical explanation of the meaning of U.S. history is Frederick Jackson Turner's frontier theory. His popular and persuasive arguments stressed the importance of the untamed land in shaping a new culture, a new spirit, for all the American people. Turner's thesis has been chewed over, challenged, even ridiculed, but it still grips the imagination, as the persistence of the "western" in American movies and popular literature demonstrates.

The frequency with which Americans move during their lifetimes (greater than in any other country) reflects the psychological compulsion—or perhaps biological necessity—of Americans to move on from their place of birth and place of employment to new places in the search for new opportunities. The importance of the automobile—and other forms of transportation—in American life highlights this emphasis on movement.

Even the special sense of place attached to California reflects the continuing power of the westward movement. In the minds of many, California represents the ultimate goal, the "land's end" beyond which movement cannot continue. Californians, celebrating their status of having arrived at the ultimate goal, validate the concept of the westward movement.

The accompanying photographs show that the process of moving west (with all its implications of dream and reality) was a goal of virtually all classes and all races among those newly arrived from across the Atlantic. The significant exception was, of course, the native American, whose much earlier arrival from the other end of the Eurasian land mass had permitted his descendants to achieve a gradual adjustment to place. The Indian (as he was to become known to the later comers) was able to achieve both a religious and economic commitment to places increasingly perceived as home and identified with the graves of his ancestors. It is not surprising that the bustling, future-oriented recent immigrants from across the Atlantic almost inevitably clashed with the descendants of the traditional-minded immigrants from the other direction.

Had there been no native inhabitants when Columbus opened up the New World to Europeans and Africans, the history of the United States might have been no more exciting or morally illuminating than a gigantic real estate sale. But, because of the prior existence of a people with different values, the history of the United States is one of moral ambiguity, military conflict, and psychological intensity.

The movement west shown in these photographs covers nearly every form of locomotion known to man: the human leg, the horse, the mule, the railroad, the sailing ship. The twentieth century has substituted more efficient forms of locomotion for those of the nineteenth century, but the new kinds continue to reflect the historical and psychological imperative of "moving on."

Because the United States is a democratic society, the movement west was chaotic as well as vigorous. Good and bad are often visible side by side as, for example, a school and an opium den. Such contrasts are less evident in Canada, whose government exerted more control over the movement. Canadians and Americans will no doubt continue to argue over the comparative virtues of their two societies and over the judgment of history with regard to their differing pasts.

And always the Indian: the conscience of America, his or her impassive face gazing out at the intruder, wondering what the future has in store. And, as we gaze back, we ask the same question.

Wilcomb E. Washburn

With the westward expansion, the United States became conscious of itself as a nation with two coastlines and major ports to match. New Bedford, Massachusetts, immortalized by Herman Melville in *Moby Dick,* began as a whaling port in 1765, reaching its peak less than a hundred years later in 1857 when it could boast 329 whaling ships. Opposite, during 1890, New Bedford docks are still covered with casks of whale oil, a lamp fuel soon to be replaced by petroleum. San Francisco ships plied the Pacific trade or rounded the Horn to Europe and the States. William Shew's 1852 panorama of daguerreotypes, below, reveals barks and barkentines in various states of decay, abandoned by their sailors, who jumped ship at Frisco to go a-moiling for gold. Statehood came in 1850.

Carleton E. Watkins (1829-1916), first in a line of great Far-West documentary landscapists, captured the mood of the California wilderness. Left, a hunter stands in front of the "Grizzly Giant," a conifer with a 33-foot diameter (1861). Top, a Watkins portrayal of Yosemite. For a rare view of miners in the diggings, above, Watkins visited John C. Frémont's 40,000-acre estate (1860).

Leland Stanford's Central Pacific Railroad and Thomas Durant's Union
Pacific meet in 1869, at right, moments
before the oft-pictured ceremony with
the golden spike at Promontory Summit,
Utah. With boots and saddle, ex-slave
and notable cowboy Nat Love, alias
Deadwood Dick, poses in his rodeo
get-up, opposite. He ended his days
riding the trains, an employee of the
Pullman Company. Throughout the
nineteenth century the Plains tribes had
resisted the advance of the settlers. In
August 1862, Sioux chief Little Crow
led a massacre of 800 white settlers
along the Minnesota River northwest of
Mankato. Top, exhausted survivors rest
on the prairie. With the end of the Civil
War in 1865, the United States directed
its military might westward. Within a
generation the U.S. Army had crushed
armed Indian resistance.

Civilian mule drivers balance casks of provisions. They and their animals helped to provide logistical support for the cavalry units of General Crook, whose successful counterattack helped avenge the massacre of George Custer and his men at Little Bighorn. The Indian warriors, superb fighting men, could not hope to win against the mass of men and supplies that an industrial nation could put into the field.

Battle Was Lost
But the War Was Won

Lt. Col. George Armstrong Custer was definitely the loser. ("General Custer" referred to his Civil War brevet rank.) In 1874, Custer precipitated a crisis in the northern plains by taking a reconnaissance expedition into forbidden Sioux treaty lands of South Dakota's Black Hills. Expedition wagons line up for inspection, opposite. And at left, Custer celebrates a bear kill. Custer reported that there was gold in those hills, whereupon a rush was on to the sacred hunting grounds. The Sioux assembled 3,000 mounted warriors for a final, climactic battle. Custer called together his officers—several of whom are shown above, with their ladies, at Fort Abraham Lincoln—and led 600 men to the Little Bighorn in Montana Territory during July 1876. The disastrous "last stand" convinced Congress to take back the ceded Black Hills. General George Crook engaged the Sioux with all the forces he could muster.

Breaking of the Power of the Plains Indian

The encampment at left was part of a huge gathering of 4,000 Sioux on White Clay Creek, near the South Dakota-Nebraska border. The village was established during January 1891 in defiance of the U.S. Army after the reckless slaughter of hundreds of Indian men, women, and children at nearby Wounded Knee. (There the Hotchkiss guns shot their bodies into so many pieces the remains had to be buried in a common grave.) But the new encampment was soon surrounded by 3,500 jittery, well-armed troopers. General Nelson Miles was able to avert further bloodshed, but this proud people would never rise again, as suggested by the evocative studio portrait of a Sioux man and woman, taken by turn-of-the century New York photographer Gertrude Käsebier. Some viewers sense resignation in the set of the woman's face: others are touched by her calm, almost kindly expression as she places her hand on her husband's shoulder. The man is composed, too, his brow clear, the mouth impassively closed, as if in acceptance of an immutable historic fact. But the eyes burn.

Pacification was not sufficient. Yankees yearned to transform the Indians into proper god-fearing "Americans." Promising youths were selected to study agriculture at Virginia's Hampton Institute. Top, the "before" picture of the very first class (1878), left to right and back row: Laughing Face, an Arikara; White Breast, a Mandan; Carries Flying, a Blackfoot Sioux; Man Who Looks Around, a Mandan; and Sioux Boy (Ka-ru-nack), an Arikara. Second row, left to right: Sharphorn, tribe unknown; Walking Cloud, a Hunkpapa Sioux (Sitting Bull's tribe); One Who Hoots When He Walks, a Hunkpapa; White Wolf, an Arikara. Front, seated: Long Arm, a Gros Ventre. Readers are on their own with the "after" photograph taken 15 months later. Left, famed athlete Jim Thorpe, of Sauk and Fox heritage, attended Carlyle Indian School in Pennsylvania.

While the Colonel Custers and General Crooks were putting down Indian insurrections, the new settlers tried to piece together a rough semblance of civilization on the western plains. And where settlers came, could schools be far behind? Schoolmarm Blanche Lamont, above, taught in Hecla, Montana (1892). Frontier schooling was better than any eastern snob would have expected—in fact, by the turn of the century Iowa, Kansas, and Nebraska had the highest literacy rates in the nation. Even so, not all the lessons of the schoolmarms were effective, as the reversed "N" in the "Dance House," opposite, attests. The stagecoach, with driver and "shotgun" carefully posed, is a contract mail carrier, which kept the towns of the frontier in touch with cities and with one another. Experts say it is empty, indicated by the fact that the rear stands high: freight would have pulled it down. The stagecoach business itself was begun in 1849 by an enterprising California mail clerk. By 1858, an overland mail and passenger route had been established between San Francisco and the railhead at St. Louis. The trip took 25 days, so long as the wheels stayed on and there were no holdups by highwaymen or attacks by Indians. The arrival of the train shortened the transcontinental crossing from a month to a week, but stage links were still required between station stops and outlying communities.

Real cowboys have always been hard to find. With their tough, dangerous and lonely lifestyle, they stayed on the range with the dogies and seldom survived beyond 40 years of age. They spawned, however, a lively art form, its showbiz apotheosis seen in the "Dodge City Cowboy Band," right, and famous crackshot Annie Oakley, opposite. Born in Ohio during 1860, brave Annie learned marksmanship in her backyard. She gained fame with the Buffalo Bill Wild West show and retired back home in Dayton. Eastern tenderfoot, Rudolf Eickemeyer, Jr., above, with his cow-pony Major, arrived in 1885 to photograph scenes along Colorado's Great Divide. He soon hurried back to Manhattan, there to win his spurs in the studio, a high-fashion photographer and darling of high society.

The Last Day

In full regalia, left, tamed Indian chiefs
assemble at Carlyle, Pennsylvania,
prior to a trip to Washington for a 1905
parade. Left to right are: Little Plume,
of the Nez Perce; Buckskin Charlie of
the Utes; Geronimo, the great Apache
warrior; Quanah Parker of the Co-
manche; Hollow Horn Bear, a Sioux;
and American Horse, a Sioux warrior.
Above, every bit the princess, sits the
grand-daughter of Cochise, feared
leader of the Chiricahua Apache. As of
this writing, her fate is unknown.

*What treaty that the white man
ever made with us have they
kept? Not one.*
—Sitting Bull

TURNING THE CENTURY

Americans had long been able to boast of bounteous resources, but labor remained in short supply until millions of unskilled European immigrants began arriving after 1850. Total population doubled between the Civil War and World War I. And during these same generations, the United States became the world's premier agricultural producer. It also moved out front in manufacturing, advancing from behind the shadow of Britain, Germany, and France.

So-called "risk capital," likewise chronically scarce in antebellum times, became abundant as foreigners invested in American railroads and other "safe" kinds of enterprise. This freed domestic funds for extractive industries and other speculative ventures. The high-rolling gamblers arrived. Leading celebrities of the age were not the statesmen, not the generals, but "captains of industry." Andrew Carnegie and John D. Rockefeller were living embodiments of the fictional characters created by Horatio Alger.

Daredevil named Dixon at Niagara, opposite, and tunnelers beneath the Hudson embodied the spirit of the 1900s.

Also accorded lofty popular status were inventors. More than half the men who occupy the upper reaches of our Historic Pantheon of Heroic Inventors flourished in the half-century between the Civil War and the World War: Edison, Bell, Westinghouse, Charles Martin Hall, Ottmar Mergenthaler, and Wilbur and Orville Wright. Of similar rank were great builders and engineers such as John A. Roebling and James B. Eads. In a unique category was Henry Ford, perhaps the only genuine revolutionary in American history. Significantly, only one political figure captured popular fancy to the same extent that Ford did. Theodore Roosevelt—"that damned cowboy," as the Ohio politico Mark Hanna called him.

By 1901, when an assassin killed Hanna's protégé William McKinley and thereby made Roosevelt president, industries created by freewheeling entrepreneurs in the 1870s and 1880s were becoming mature economic institutions. When mismanagement took its toll, as was particularly the case with railroads during the depression of the 1890s, only Wall Street commanded the resources to bail them out. Industry's vulnerability to cutthroat competition led inevitably to concentration and monopoly. J. Pierpont Morgan lent money only to enterprises he could control.

Yet, even as monopolists fell under increasing fire by President Roosevelt and the progressives, most Americans still sought to emulate them, if only in small ways. In truth, the "Robber Barons" simply reflected contemporary standards. Mark Twain, who understood that millions of his countrymen were "promoters" at heart, wrought a brilliant satire on their comportment and values in his *Gilded Age*.

For successful promoters at least, the concept of "Social Darwinism" seemed to fit the Gilded Age ideally. The rise of big business, Rockefeller said, was "merely the working-out of a law of nature and a law of God." Whether or not this worked to the general good—and we can see that the social costs of rapid industrialization were devastating—there is no doubt that the turn of the century was a time of phenomenal growth in almost every realm.

The persistent "farm problem" brought on by declining prices resulted in a shift of American attitudes toward the role of government. The problem abated temporarily toward the turn of the century, however, at the same time that farmers were being seduced by the lure of mechanization. Gasoline tractors were available from several firms by 1902, and the first successful "crawler" was patented two years later. Mechanization was the harbinger of profound change, particularly in new farming regions of the West.

An equally profound change affected American attitudes toward "frontiers" overseas. What began as a minor crusade in Cuba against a lesser military power (Spain) ended with the U.S. deeply ensconced in the Far East as well as the Caribbean. Though relatively restrained in its imperialist adventures, the nation nevertheless assumed a new stance vis-à-vis Asia and Latin America.

Yet the consequences of this new notion of manifest destiny pale in comparison to those stemming from shifting attitudes toward technology. As Henry Adams wrote in 1918 in the autobiography he called his *Education*, "the new American—the child of incalculable coal-power, chemical power, electric power, and radiating energy, as well as of new forces yet undetermined—must be a sort of God compared with any former creation of nature." The extent to which we could actually control all this power and energy would remain a vexed question, but the impact of such "new forces" is abundantly evident in the selection of photographs that follows.

Robert C. Post

In search of better traction and less damage to the soil, farm machinery designer Benjamin Holt substituted tracks for wheels. He tests the first such "crawler" in 1904 near Stockton, California. His system gained in popularity during the Great War when vehicles equipped with tracks stayed on the move while others bogged down in the mud. Fame for the "Caterpillar" was assured when the British revolutionized military operations by adopting Holt tracks for their new war wagon, the "tank." Like others of his generation, Ben Holt kept up with new technology and, in later years, took up flying.

SAFE FOR ONLY 25 MEN AT ONE
TIME. DO NOT WALK CLOSE TOGETHER.
NOR RUN. JUMP. OR TROT. BREAK
STEP!
                W. A. Roebling, Eng'r in Chief.

Bridges to Success

Opposite, in 1877 construction company directors climb the catwalk to celebrate the first wire strung on John A. Roebling's Great East River Bridge, later the Brooklyn Bridge. Page 161 shows the project a year earlier. It was completed in 1888 and, at 1,600 feet, remained the longest suspension bridge well into the 20th century. A competing approach, the cantilever span, above, takes form in St. Louis. The rigid framework of the Eads Bridge gains unusual

strength from contoured beams of steel. It excels at carrying heavy rail traffic. Top, begun in 1927, New York's George Washington Bridge employs the Roebling approach, though much perfected during half a century of practice. The basic technique involves the spiderlike spinning of cables from lengths of wire—each unrolled from a giant spool. Bundled and clamped, the parallel strands create thick cables, often several feet in cross section.

"For the first time in the history of mankind, men walked on land from New Jersey to New York." So remarks William G. McAdoo, opposite (tall man near center), with reporters and chief engineer Charles Jacobs. They attend the opening of the Hudson and Manhattan Railroad Tunnel on March 12, 1904. Though McAdoo went on to a distinguished career in politics, he was always proudest of his "McAdoo Tunnels," twin-tube bores and a system of electric commuter lines (now PATH). Above, several McAdoo "sandhogs" work in the pressurized chamber behind the Greathead Shield (see also page 109), a device enabling tunnels to be pushed under rivers. New technology spawned new hazards: until science described it in 1888, one of every four sandhogs died from Caisson's disease or "the bends," a crippling deposition of nitrogen bubbles in the blood due to conditions of high pressure.

As Big as All Outdoors

Premier mode of travel between Chicago and St. Louis at the turn of the century was the Chicago and Alton Railroad's showcase, the "Alton Limited," below. From cowcatcher to observation platform, every element of the six-car train was carefully coordinated, creating the world's first train with a designer look as well as matched machinery. To document this engineering and artistic feat, the railroad ordered a photograph made from a single negative, not pieced together from several exposures. Company photographer George A. Lawrence took ten weeks to build this camera around a frame of wooden beams, and, extended, it spanned 20 feet. Loaded with a glass plate 4.5 by eight feet, it weighed 1,400 pounds. Using its telescopic lens for the panorama shown here, a 150-second exposure was taken at Brighton Park, Illinois, on a fine spring day in 1900. This view hung for more than 70 years in the Chicago offices of the C&A and its several corporate successors—testimony to an amazing whim.

on.Co.
ENVER. Colo.

The two at left are real accidents, but the metal melee above is a spectacle—a popular if uncommon entertainment of the late 1800s. Two old locomotives, full throttle, plow into each other while thousands cheer. This demolition derby was probably staged in the Midwest, but details have been lost. Contrived or not, the big wrecks made generations of Americans shudder and gasp. There were certainly disasters enough to publicize; in 1875 alone, long after telegraphic train orders, 104 head-on collisions were recorded. A decade later, at Batavia, New York, a photographer recorded a double-decker, opposite top. How could it happen? The cause of another disaster, opposite bottom, is all-too-readily apparent: a bridge that couldn't take it. There could have been another reason, too: Americans love to push technology to the limit—heavier engines, longer trains—and sometimes something had to give. At Calvary, Kentucky, this locomotive has hit the ground like a dropped flatiron and, on the trestle, a car teeters at the edge of eternity.

At Santa Monica, J.B. Marquis and partner tip over a Sunbeam racer during the Vanderbilt Cup of 1914. Two-wheelers also provided thrills. Above, in the same year, the winner of a 100-miler strikes a victorious pose. Top, cyclist-turned-aviator Calbraith P. Rodgers seeks the big money, $50,000 for the first coast-to-coast flight in 35 days or less. He made it across, but 19 days too late for the cash. On the way he crashed 19 times.

Doll painter *c.* 1920 works in an old-fashioned factory; but the women inhabit a brave new world—the assembly line. With mechanized mass production all in place, there remained just one loose end: the workers themselves. Homogenizing their little quirks was the goal of the prophets of scientific management, Frederick W. Taylor and Frank B. Gilbreth. With wife Lillian—heroine of *Cheaper by the Dozen*—Gilbreth devised the "orbit method." Movies were taken against a super-imposed grid. The worker's wired ring flashed. Many twists and turns indicated too much "waste motion" and many flashes indicated too much "wasted time." The notion that there was only one best way to perform a task reflected what labor regarded as management's urge to dehumanize the work force.

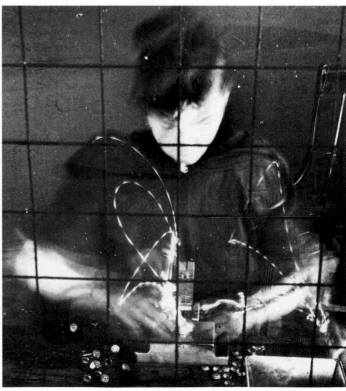

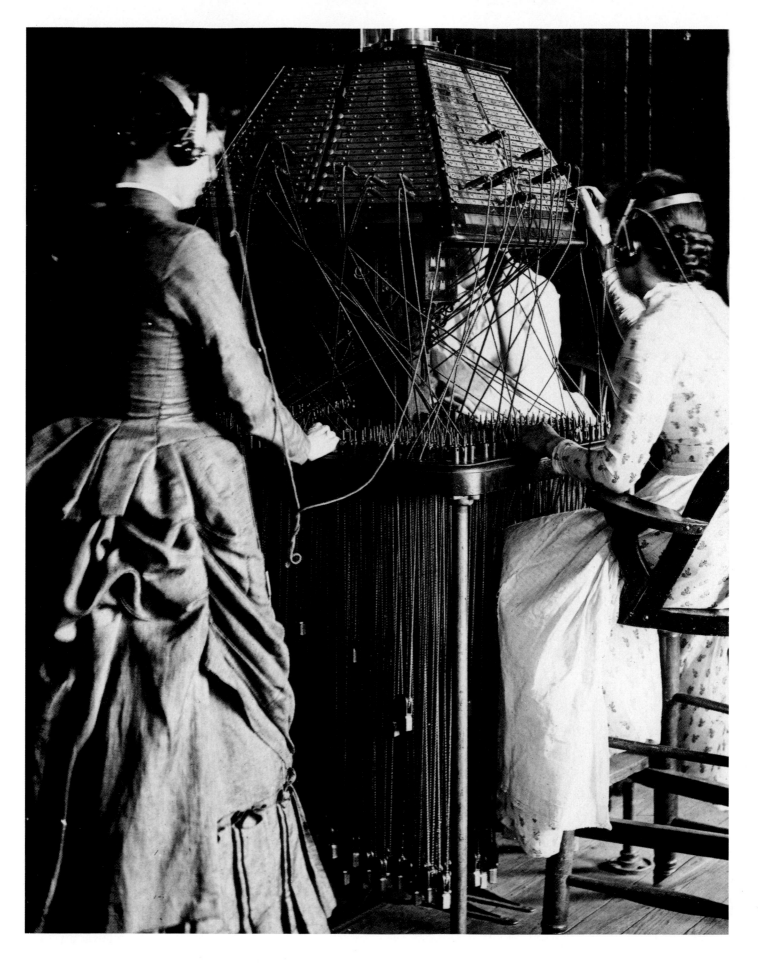

Ma Bell and Women's Work

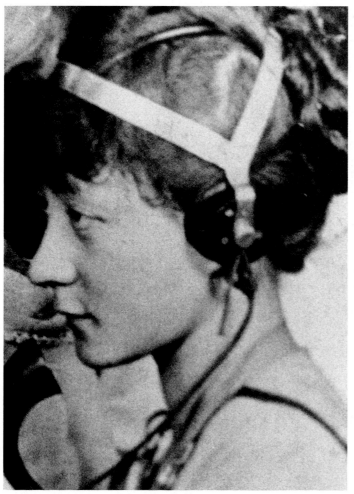

Tangled switchboard lines nearly strangled the infant telephone industry. And as interesting as the many technical fixes were (including, opposite, the lampshade style of 1882 in Richmond, Virginia), even more significant was a social shift evident in each of these pictures. Although boys had been hired as operators originally, by the turn of the century that occupation was firmly fixed in people's minds as women's work. The supervisor with her dozens of "girls" became part of the culture. Through equipment standardization and the hiring of bevies of young women, the switchboard bottleneck was broken. The result: from 1.3 million telephones in 1900, the system expanded to 10.5 million sets by 1915— one phone for every ten people in the United States.

Fanfare for the Uncommon Woman

From the frontier to the footlights, American women aspired to great things, but they often ended up type-cast. The ladylike ensemble here demonstrates the new competence that women were able to attain and assert at the beginning of the new century, a period of rapid social and economic turnover. Both an artistic and an economic success, the Helen May Butler organization stayed on the road for 55 consecutive weeks during the 1903 season, their most triumphant. But Mrs. Butler had another note to strike for gender independence: in 1936 she ran a spirited race for the U.S. Senate. Not winning—hardly expecting to—she said that she had been motivated by a strong desire to pave the way for future female candidates.

Often Sung But Seldom Seen

Editor's Note: The decades before and after 1900 were a golden age of invention and new-product introduction. Corporations began to shape their identities. But behind famous product names, services, and organizations, we always find extraordinary people—original American self-starters. *Images* book staff researchers worked at length to assemble this collection of authentic overachievers. We trust that the reader will find the same delight we did in seeing the faces behind so many famous household names and national institutions.

1. King Camp Gillette

4. Clara Barton

5. J. L. Kraft

6. Henry J. Heinz

9. Richard W. Sears

10. Alvah C. Roebuck

11. John B. Stetson

3. John S. Pemberton

2. Milton S. Hershey

7. Milton Bradley

8. Mary Ann Magnin

12. Levi Strauss

13. George S. Parker

1. **King Camp Gillette** thought of his safety razor in 1895. It featured a disposable, two-edged blade.

2. **Milton S. Hershey**, "the man behind the candy bar," created his chocolate company after 1903.

3. **John S. Pemberton**, an Atlanta druggist, developed the secret formula for Coca-Cola in 1886.

4. **Clara Barton** founded the American Red Cross in 1881.

5. **J. L. Kraft** started a wholesale cheese business in 1903 and patented a method for processing cheese in 1916.

6. **Henry J. Heinz** started his successful food-preserving company in 1876.

7. **Milton Bradley** transformed his lithographic press into a producer of popular parlor games after 1860.

8. **Mary Ann Magnin** founded the I. Magnin department store of San Francisco in 1876.

9. **Richard W. Sears** started out selling watches in 1886 and joined forces with A. C. Roebuck a year later.

10. **Alvah C. Roebuck** sold out his interests in 1924, but returned to the company later.

11. **John B. Stetson** started making felt hats in 1865. Quality and style—often with a western flair—turned his product into an American institution.

12. **Levi Strauss** developed Levi's® blue jeans during the California gold-rush and started a legend.

13. **George S. Parker** incorporated the Parker Pen Company in Janesville, Wisconsin, in 1892.

Fresh Faces of the New Century

Sixteen pages at the United States Capitol probably mirror the demeanor, if not the attitudes, of the nation's elected lawmakers. These lads ran errands for the Senators during 1904. Then, politics was a man's world, and women voted only in Wyoming, Utah, Idaho, and Colorado and never ran for office. In an age of unusually high male self-esteem, some pages surely would have felt entitled to public office. Some may have made it— we'll probably never know. The facts are scattered in family albums all across the country.

132

From the trooper on his Morgan pony in the Wild West, top, to our lads in the Philippines, opposite, the American fighting man served an assertive people. The nation clamored to consolidate its territory at home and extend its influence abroad. Foreign involvement began in a big way on February 15, 1898, with the sinking of the battleship *Maine* in Havana harbor. In a "splendid little war," Theodore Roosevelt and Admiral George Dewey became popular heroes. The name of another paragon has languished, though. Lt. Col. Andrew Summers Rowan, left, plunged into Cuba after military intelligence. His exploits became legend in Elbert Hubbard's essay "A Message to Garcia."

On to the Heavens

Theodore Roosevelt, right, settles into a Wright biplane with pilot Arch Hoxey during 1910. TR's trip both thrilled and troubled the country. In 1911 alone, 100 fliers died in mishaps. Harriet Quimby, opposite, America's flying sweetheart, fell to her death in 1912. Yet aviation was advancing, and on January 1, 1914, a photographer recorded quite an event: inauguration of scheduled, commercial air service in the United States (probably in the world, too) by the St. Petersburg–Tampa Airboat Line, above. Passenger A.C. Pheil poses between the company's organizer, Percival Fansler (on the left), and the pilot of its Benoist Type XIV flying boat, Tony Jannus.

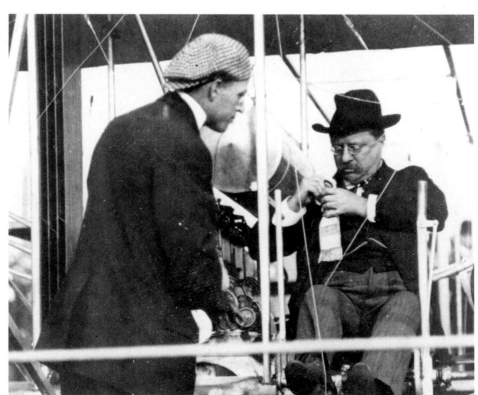

In Fighting Trim

By the opening years of the 20th century there was no doubt that the United States had emerged as one of the world's premier powers. Theodore Roosevelt personified that power. His penchant for striking poses such as the one with the huge globe testified to a singular flair for the dramatic, top. Far more effective testimony, though, was the "Great White Fleet," 16 warships with 12,000 men aboard, which he dispatched at the end of 1907. Here we view the front of the long column, led by the U.S.S. *New Jersey*. In one of the most memorable shows of muscle in all history—the intended audience mostly Japan—the fleet sailed world sea-lanes until February 1909, when TR left office. In his autobiography, Theodore Roosevelt called the Great White Fleet "the most important service that I rendered to peace."

Whether they will or no, Americans must begin to look outward.
— Alfred Thayer Mahan (1897)

PART THREE
AMERICA—A FAMILY AFFAIR

Joe Goodwin

Everybody knows something about the social glue that holds America together—our wider allegiances to the big national family. But the immediate family, with its roots and our interfamily affiliations, is most important in terms of the most extraordinary experience, that great but often underrated adventure called everyday life. Photography can capture its surface. We urge the reader, though, to practice looking not simply "at" a picture but "in" a picture. Sometimes, by peering deep into a photograph's "mirror of life," we can actually pass through the looking glass to a more perfect experience and appreciate our beginnings, and even our endings.

Take the present example. Black or white, many southerners born before 1950 will be able to read volumes in the face of the person at left. Born in slave times, he was known simply as Uncle Essick, yet he represents a social watershed, the first generation of free Blacks in what was Old Dixie. Curiously, it took a Yankee to catch the wary and resilient spark in his eye. In 1890, Rudolf Eickemeyer, Jr., visited Mt. Meigs, Alabama, and in bright vision captured bits of the life of one little group of sharecroppers. (See also pages 26 and 27.) Returning to New York City, Eickemeyer went on to become his day's most celebrated society and glamour photographer. The pictures were published later in book form, called *Down South*, with an introduction by Joel Chandler Harris, creator of the character Uncle Remus.

Just what, then, does this wonderful portrait reveal: what is meant by that light in the old gentleman's eye? Did Eickemeyer's professional brilliance somehow contaminate the real meaning of Uncle Essick's life and experience? Yes, the artist's skill and commercial instincts most certainly changed some things—prettied them up and made them picturesque—yet for many viewers the inner strength of his subject really does shine through. And that is precisely what makes great photographs great. With care and luck, the interpretation of historic photos for social meaning, even for personal significance, can be successful. It is often attempted on these pages: with what degree of success each reader must individually decide. No easy task, for many subjective factors come into play.

"America, A Family Affair" may be the book's most subjective part, for it deals with the ties that bind. Blest be they, and blest be the changes that inevitably soften, modify, or even overcome strict, old-line loyalties and allegiances. It happens in any setting that nurtures a vital social experiment. Where more so than in America?

Not surprisingly, we suggest that in the United States all our social adhesive takes on a family form. In fact, as America's great geographic expanse holds one nation made up of several "nations," so our one big fam-

Preceding pages: A man who has known both slavery and freedom, "Uncle Essick" relaxes in the postbellum South of 1894. These pages: Through humor, homeless survivors overcome calamity in the wake of the earthquake that leveled much of San Francisco in 1906. With special glasses, or stereoscopes, viewers could blend two nearly identical photographs to create a single illusion of deep three-dimensionality: the hologram of its day. In the inset photograph (also one-half of a stereograph), a family enjoys stereography in an English parlor, c. 1860. Come be a "spectator to the best views the world had to offer," wrote Oliver Wendell Holmes, extolling the virtues of the stereograph just before the Civil War. Holmes later modified the design of the hand-held stereoscope and created a practical instrument still in use today.

ily is composed of many "families" and ties. Of course, these change over time. Some family ties derive from the basics: blood, history, and geography. Others are more ephemeral, involving neighborhoods in transition, vocational associations, education and income levels, or even the strange bedfellows that politics makes.

If the viewer and reader is curious and brave, there is simply no reason to hesitate. Why not take up a few family photographs and attempt to assign, as Shakespeare put it, "a local habitation and a name" to all the many nuclear and extended familial affinities that your pictured ancestor so prized and, in the end, may have found challenged. Photo albums will provide many clues.

Beyond the people they contain, usually the main subjects, our pictures include settings that may reveal unexpected insight into our family heritage and how it has changed, or remained stable, over the decades. Since the camera can "remember" everything it "sees," we find a wealth of fascinating detail. In this pursuit, a sort of game can be played. It tests how perceptive and observant we are, and it involves only three people. In form, it is a variant of the famous "Kim's Game" in Rudyard Kipling's spy novel *Kim*.

Two individuals do the looking, searching into the background. One player quizzes the two observers. He asks, for instance, "What time was it when the picture was taken? There was a clock on the wall; did you notice its make?" The game can go on indefinitely, especially if the scene in question was, say, a country store. All the more meaningful if it was your grandfather's country store. If you really get into the game, at the end of an hour you may well know what was on sale in the store, what each person was wearing, and that the calico cat was lying near a Ben Franklin stove. You may also grow increasingly curious about things in the picture you never even noticed before.

After a while, all the bright little bits of evidence converge—as if of their own volition—and then you've really put yourself inside the picture. Go outside the game and ask the right person, and perhaps you will even find out the name of the calico cat.

If you don't have a family album, ask relatives to let you see theirs, and perhaps copy some prints or negatives. But if you look in the attic or under the stairs you'll find some old snapshots of your own. In the meantime, a good place to start learning how to uncover the ins and outs of your own family history, discovering secrets and surprises from the past, is to go a-voyaging in time through this book, America's photo album.

Welcome to the really big family!

141

THE PROMISED LAND

We Americans have never had much doubt as to what sets us apart from other peoples of the world. The Revolutionary War was still in progress when J. Hector St. John Crèvecoeur described the new nation as a "great American asylum," where "the poor of Europe have by some means met together."

"What then is this American," he asked, "this new man?"

He is either an European or the descendent of an European; hence that strange mixture of blood which you will find in no other country. I could point out to you a family whose grandfather was an Englishman, whose wife was Dutch, whose son married a French woman, and whose present four sons have now four wives of different nations. *He* is an American who, leaving behind him all his ancient prejudices and manners, receives new ones from the new mode of life he has embraced.

The author allowed a few of his own "new" preju-

dices to show. He might have noted that Americans came in two sexes, and, for the moment, three races. Crèvecoeur included the "English, Scotch, Irish, French, Dutch, Germans and Swedes" in his recipe for the "promiscuous American brew," but he ignored the native Americans—already being pushed out of the way and onto greater or lesser trails of tears. Nor did he mention those unwilling emigrants who arrived in chains from Angola, the Gold Coast, the Windward Coast, Senegambia, Sierra Leone, and the Bights of Biafra and Benin.

From the outset, racial, social, and cultural diversity has been both the source of our greatest strength and the root of our fundamental national problem. In 1621 an officer of the Virginia Company, anxious to strengthen Jamestown industry, dispatched a party of Italian glassblowers to the colony. A member of the welcoming committee took one look and declared, "A more damn'd crew Hell never vomited."

Those Italian craftsmen were among the first "greenhorns," pioneering a route to be followed by the millions of emigrants who would forge a new nation with their intelligence, their muscle, and their skillful hands. They were the first of the "strangers," forced to deal

---

Maronite Christian girl from the Holy Land, her family settled in Detroit, tends a Palm Sunday candle. Opposite, Rom Gypsy woman of Central European origin.

with the hostility of those who had come before them.

A century later, Benjamin Franklin echoed the response of his Virginia predecessor. "Why," he asked, "should the Palatine Boors be suffered to swarm into our Settlements and, by herding together, establish their Language and Manners, to the Exclusion of ours? Why should Pennsylvania, founded by the English, become a Colony of *Aliens*, who will shortly be so numerous as to Germanize us, instead of our Anglifying them, and will never adopt our Language or Customs any more than they can acquire our Complexion."

Succeeding generations of Americans shared Franklin's sentiments, but they also faced the problems of building canals and railroads, operating factories, and opening a continent. The profound and deeply rooted fear of being overwhelmed by foreign hordes was more than offset by the desire to take full advantage of cheap emigrant labor.

And so they came, wave after wave, from Germany, Ireland, Scandinavia, Central, Southern and Eastern Europe, Asia, and Latin America. The United States of America was the Promised Land, the universal destination for those who were driven from their homes by economic hardship and political oppression. No one really believed that the streets of New York or San Francisco were paved with gold. Few were so naive as to suppose that they would be welcomed with open arms. What they did expect was opportunity, and they found it.

Every emigrant who has struggled to preserve precious traditions and memories while accommodating to a new environment has, in America, discovered the sensation of being trapped between two worlds. American culture is enormously richer for this experience— ironically, a liberating experience.

Walt Whitman summed it up over a century ago. America, he said, is "not merely a nation, but a teeming nation of nations." We are a product of the talent and energy of people who have come here from around the globe, bringing with them the challenge of new ideas and a determination to realize the dream of a better life for themselves and their fellow citizens.

Tom Crouch

Hearts filled with hope, smiling Slavic immigrants greet the New World at New York's Ellis Island in 1905.

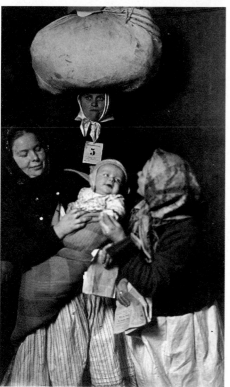

On a latter-day *Mayflower*, opposite, passage to America might cost $12. All newcomers faced momentary anxiety at such portals as Ellis Island in New York Harbor, through which the Slav family, left, and six million other immigrants passed during the first decade of the 20th century. Medical examinations awaited: while the vast majority passed, many were rejected. Top, a Hebraic eye-chart and stethoscope help immigration officials examine Jewish immigrants. Indignities were brief, with inspectors primarily on the lookout for infectious diseases.

The Sicilian woman carrying her garment piecework, top, and peasant farmer turned steelworker, above, were photographed in 1909 by Lewis W. Hine, pioneer of the "photo story."

Italians on American Shores:

Italian fishermen tend their fishing boat on the beach at Monterey, California, in 1889. Few Italian immigrants, however, were lucky enough to build lives in the countryside, though most emigrated from rural areas south of Rome and from the fields and groves of Sicily. Though unaccustomed to city life, the newcomers settled in the Eastern cities where most available jobs were concentrated, forming enclaves known as "Little Italys" to help perpetuate family unity. So many immigrated during the early 1900s that more Italians lived in New York than in Rome.

150

Sanctuary on America's Western Doorsteps

A Chinese congregation, left, gathers outside a church in Honolulu. Driven by famine, flood, war, and lured by tales of gold, Chinese began a large-scale emigration to America during the 1850s. In 1882, however, growing anti-Chinese sentiment in California boiled over, and the Chinese Exclusion Act was passed, closing the nation's borders. By then, the transcontinental railroads were completed and thousands of Chinese Americans experienced discrimination as they competed for jobs with "white" Americans. Taking advantage of the labor shortages, Japanese emigration increased. Top, thoroughly Americanized by the 1930s, having children born in the States, a stylish woman poses for a portrait just before her first return visit to the land of her birth. She came to the United States from Japan after 1900 for a marriage arranged by her own family and another. Overall, as United States borders became fixed, the country began to define itself by establishing immigration quotas to limit the numbers of entrants from individual countries.

Hispanic Americans

Long before North European settlers and homesteaders arrived, the ancestors of such Hispanic families as the Lugos of Bell, California, right, owned ranches throughout the Southwest. One proud community, a century and a half older than the United States, still thrives in New Mexico. Skilled Mexican horsemen were the forerunners of American cowboys—the word "buckaroo" derives from *vaquero*, the Mexican term for cowboy. Until the 1920s, Mexican workers passed freely back and forth across the loosely patrolled border seeking higher wages. Many came illegally—in some years more than a million entered the country. Two gaunt-faced Hispanic migrants are portrayed, above, in 1974.

Early in the 20th century, young Cherokee Indians of North Carolina perform a ritual dance prior to a lacrosse game, left. The sport, known to some Indians as "little brother of war," was adapted into a gentler version by European settlers and survives as a popular collegiate sport. North America's original occupants, with their myriad nations and cultures, had developed complex political organizations, religions, and languages. A Tlingit woman of the Pacific Northwest, above, displays the careful symmetry of basket design. The collision of Indian culture with European brought the decline of the former, though to this day Indians universally honor their heritage.

First Americans

Seeking harmony with the land, the seasons, and the ways of their ancestors, Hopi Indians assemble for a bean planting ceremony at Walpi Pueblo in Arizona during the 1890s. The costumed figures represent Kachinas, the spirits who watch over Hopi—the name of both the people and their ancestral territory. The community considers itself among the oldest in the United States, having inhabited the same lands for more than a thousand years.

. . . the land was alive to his loving touch, and he, its son, was brother to all creatures.
—Stewart Udall

LITTLE OL' NEW YORK
ET AL

Vertical exaggeration Manhattan style, opposite (1935). Top, blue-collar acrobat helps to build the Empire State Building, completed in 1931.

What Everest is to mountains, New York is to cities, that is, the absolute pinnacle. Hometown of the skyscraper and every and all other superlatives, and it was what other cities wanted to be when they grew up. At least that's how I thought of it there as a kid in the thirties, and me with the ultimate urban mountaineering gear: a few nickels and dimes and lots of press passes, the "crème de la crème" of keys to the city. These last came from Helen, my mother, a rising light in the publishing industry.

Early on I learned what it felt like to be on top of the world. You see, if something was really big our magnetic town attracted it and so the immense German airship *Hindenburg* logically made New York a port of call. My mother was given press passes to a short "show-and-tell tour" on the ship around the city, and though she couldn't make the trip, I could. Even at sev-

eral miles' distance this thing was simply *huge*, nearly as big as the Empire State Building itself, yet still one up on it: a skyscraper cannot fly! Looking up at it from the ground below, I was awed by its incredible enormity. Yet once on board—inside it—I was charmed by its quiet and graceful style of navigation and the views were stunning of the Jersey beaches. I remember exchanging waves with smiling people below, almost close enough to touch, it seemed. And there was a *grand piano* in the passenger lounge—a *lounge* as big as one in a hotel. I was too young to take it all in, but to this day I know that *this* is the *only* way to fly!

My mother's earliest editorial offices were located upstairs from the "4-40 Club," a bar and restaurant run by one of Helen's friends, one Ole Olson. He and his partner were currently the sold-out rave top bananas of Broadway's "Olson & Johnson's Hellzapoppin," a very vaudevillian routine that was a laugh a minute for a buck or two. Helen took me to see this mad show, and midway through the many maniacal routines Olson came to stage front and loudly announced that he had a special birthday gift for the young man in "seat M-112—

from Dr. Raymond Ditmars, curator of reptiles, at the Bronx Zoo!" In those days Dr. Ditmars was well known and his name was synonymous with *snake*. Suddenly a giant klieg light poured a ring of Miami-strength sunlight around seat M-112—and this very young, very startled youth was dead center in the beam. Of course it was all a put-up job but I was ecstatic about it!

Olson, big as a blimp himself, bounded down from the stage and presented a writhing bag to me and managed to whisper over the hubbub, "Best you keep this closed until after the show. But come backstage then: I want you to trot this thing through the girls' dressing rooms with me!"

My last bit on theater, here, concerns a remarkable happening in the mid '40s. And remember as you read that this really happened—and in Carnegie Hall! And to a packed house:

One Florence Foster Jenkins put on a one-woman show in which this elderly and utterly ingratiating genteel lady stood on stage, dressed in gorgeous but matronly attire—complete with a set of full-scale angel's wings "sprouting" from her shoulders. She then proceeded to sing such taxing coloratura musical numbers as "The Queen of the Night" from Mozart's *The Magic Flute* and "Bell Song" from *Lakmé* by Delibes. These are attempted only by the most advanced, fearsomely accomplished vocalists. A magnificent pianist, appropriately named Cosme McMoon, accompanied her.

The audience cheered lustily after each number. A few reviewers who chanced to be present—and after finally getting into the "spirit" of it all—wrote rave reviews that spoke to this audience's enthusiasm, elaborated in great detail about what Ms. Jenkins wore, the size of the house, McMoon's amazing skill at instantly transposing keys and in mid passage, but nary a word was written about Ms. Jenkins's vocal contributions.

McMoon had to be facile because Florence Foster Jenkins couldn't carry a tune in the proverbial bucket—and *didn't*! Yet tickets were in great demand among "real music lovers." For the uninitiated, like me, it was a scene right out of *Alice in Wonderland*. But it happened. It happened, in New York City, on October 25, 1944. It could happen *only* in New York City, with its infinite capacity, whatever the cost, for enjoying itself—come what may!

Of course, the city had entertainment for the masses. While a trip up Fifth Avenue was nowhere near so exciting as a nickel ride on the Staten Island Ferry, it was nonetheless a bargain of an outing. For here the buses were of the open-top variety—just like famous double-decker omnibuses of London fame. For a thin dime you hustled on board in the "Village," scampered up the spiral staircase at the rear, scooted up the aisle and plonked down in the front seat under the skies for the journey of a thousand surprises.

One of my fondest memories involves Third Avenue. I was privileged to encounter a lively remnant of a vigorous earlier period of city life. Here I saw my first and only street organ, complete with a foreign-looking man cranking the hurdy-gurdy and his dolled up, liveried

monkey holding out its paw for donations. And from this noisy box came the strains of "East Side, West Side, All Around the Town" and "Sweet Rosie O'Grady," delightfully off key, à la Florence Foster Jenkins!

New York City has changed and is going to continue to change and change again. Manhattan Island is already almost an archeological treasure chest. Yet the city may find the passing of "the ties that bind" the most lamentable loss—and the most affecting. That old-fashioned "social glue" that kept this wonderful place together is still holding, but delamination sometimes seems to lie just around the corner.

Many still view New York City in the historical mirror provided by many of the photographs in this chapter. Some people feel more comfortable with the past—and their memories of it—and perhaps prefer unconsciously to believe that that's how it really is. But I think it best we enjoy these pictures knowing that they speak to a time—not really so long ago—but a time that, sadly, is not with us now. Vanished are the neighborhood organ grinders, cranking out the warm and reassuring tunes that we use as clues to what we'd like to think New York City is—but just really isn't anymore. I know it's a real shame, but the children no longer scatter and dance to the tunes of the hurdy-gurdy man and there is pretty strong evidence that, alas, Sweet Rosie O'Grady is gone.

John Hoke

Big bustling youngster during the nation's 100th birthday, in 1876, Manhattan's "Downtown" rises behind a lone pylon of the Brooklyn Bridge-to-be. *New York Times* delights an unknown city father, above (c. 1900).

Bell telephone construction linemen of 1889, some just off the boat with their karakuls and other foreign caps, work in gangs to hook up subscribers before 1894, the year Bell's patents expire. Service costs $100 a year, and 240,000 phones were installed by 1892. The first 21 sets had been connected in New Haven only 14 years earlier.

New Yorkers of the late 1800s worked feverishly to build and rebuild their city— the labor fueled by food from soup kitchens and ethnic markets, below in a Berenice Abbot photo. Horse-drawn trolleys transport people down broad avenues during the 1880s. Top, an Alfred Stieglitz photo shows the trolley turnaround in 1893. A decade earlier, left, wires hummed overhead on Broadway and long-distance phone service ran as far as Boston. The blizzard of 1888 wreaked havoc with the web of wire, and phone and power lines soon went underground forever.

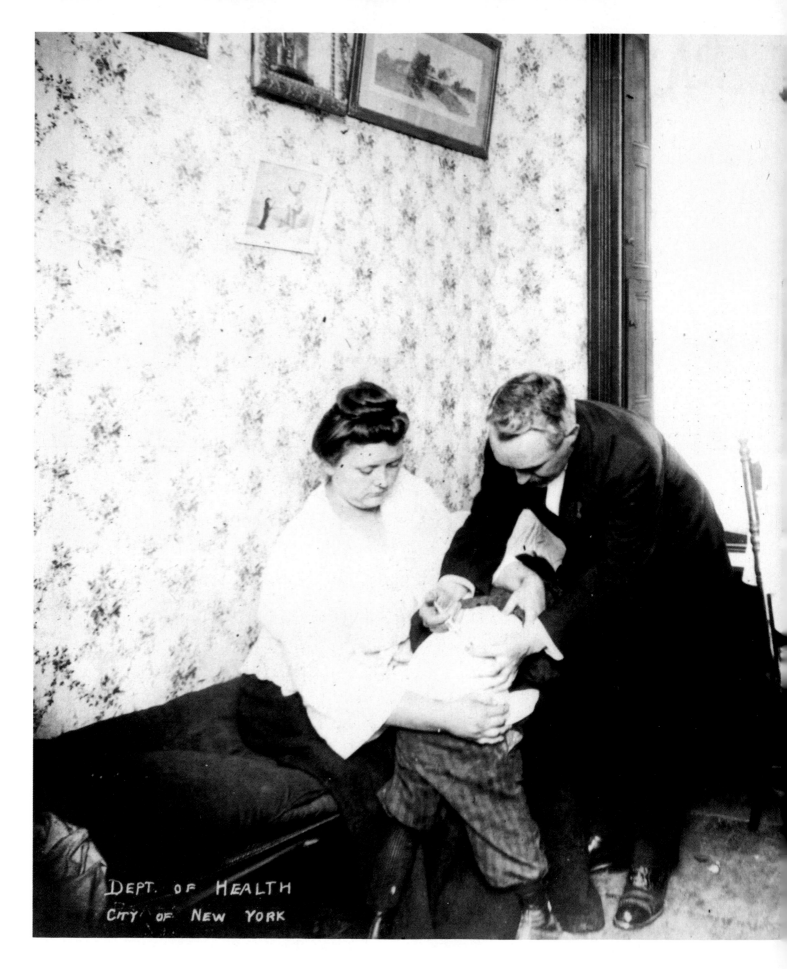

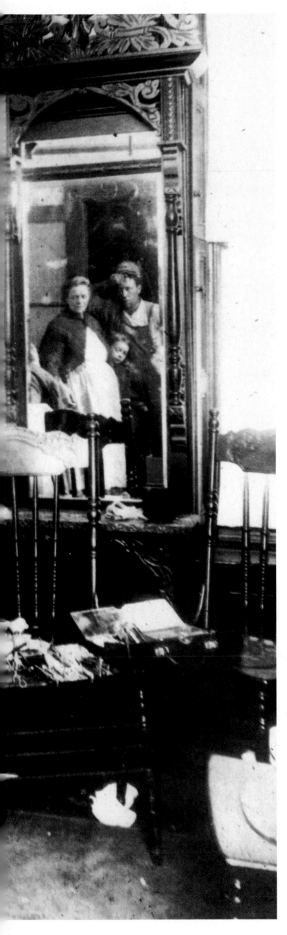

Taking Care

Epidemics of typhus and diphtheria so wracked New York that the city's Board of Health established the world's first research laboratory for infectious diseases in 1892. America's first diphtheria antitoxin was developed here: a doctor immunizes a boy, opposite, in 1920. Children suffered most from poverty and disease. In 1908, Lewis Hine captured the image of this barefoot newspaper boy, left. Reformers helped bring improvement, as with model tenements built in 1890.

Keeping Up-To-Date

Sweet Rosie O'Grady doubtless learned
to bathe babies at a class held by the
Little Mother's League. Tenement side-
walks were often the scene of these
child-care lessons, above and right, that
occurred throughout the city just after
1900. Lewis Hine photographed a
young immigrant girl, top, on the East
Side in 1905. Whatever New York's big
problems—clean water and sanitation
were certainly among them—New
Yorkers tackled them in a big way, and
often first. City codes and techniques
often set the style in social reform for
cities all across the nation.

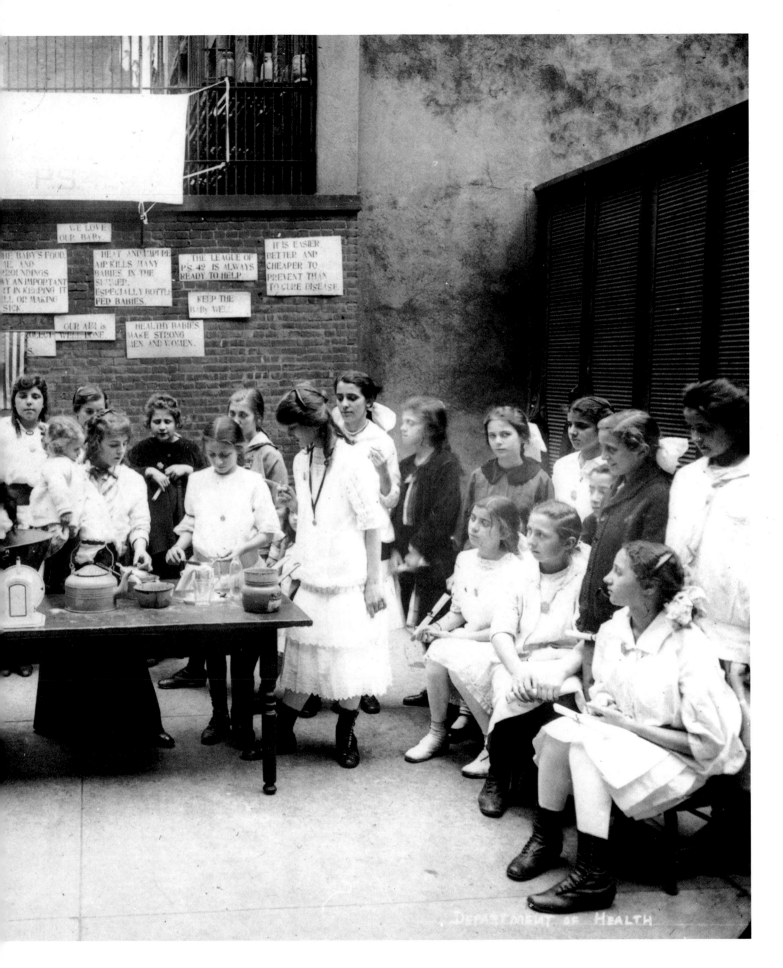

The Other Half

As the city of contrasts prospered, wealth began to attract wealth. Rocke-fellers, Vanderbilts, Astors, and others built mansions at the Battery, on upper Fifth Avenue, and Lafayette Street, their lives insulated from the harsh realities of street and slum. A mother and her daughters take tea in elegance around 1898, opposite. Top, Sarah Caffin, mother of art critic Charles Caffin (a friend of photographer Alfred Stieglitz) conserves her strength a-bed. Rich and poor both become ill, of course, but the medicine always goes down a bit easier from the silver spoon of one's own private nurse, left from 1907.

Toward the Sky

Inventor, industrialist, and philanthropist, Peter Cooper created the Cooper Union for the Advancement of Science and Art in 1853. At the junction of Third and Fourth Avenues in the Bowery, the Union's five-story structure, above, was built with wrought-iron rails perfected by Cooper for use on his railroad. Many believe that the Cooper Union building represents the earliest use of horizontal, metal I-beams in a masonry structure—the pioneering technique that made skyscrapers possible. Chicago claims the first skyscraper, the Home Insurance Building. It attained 10 stories by 1885. In 1902, the Flatiron Building at Broadway and Fifth Avenue soared to 20 stories.

The sleek Greyhound bus terminal was brand-new in 1936, opposite. Eagle-guarded Pennsylvania Station rises in the background. An incredible maze of tunnels runs beneath buildings and city streets. Left, pneumatic tubes bring 1929 Christmas mail to the main post office from as far away as Brooklyn. Top, the city's first subway, also pneumatic, was built under Broadway in 1870; the work done in secret to avoid interference from a corrupt City Hall. Eventually forgotten, the tunnel and its little car were rediscovered in 1912 by workers digging the BMT subway. Firemen, below left, depend on both air and water pumped in from a distance. New Yorkers, having built their own exotic environment, learned to put technology to work to help them cope with their creation.

The style of Alfred Stieglitz shines through: the view from his balcony at the Shelton (1907); self-portrait (1907), top; and two studies of his protégée and wife Georgia O'Keeffe, (1918) opposite, and (1918) above left. Her elegant hands transformed the art world during eight decades; at first she painted scenes from the city, where Stieglitz spent most of his career. In later years she found inspiration in the desert West. Pictures on these pages appear through special permission of the estate and the National Gallery of Art and belong to a key set of Stieglitz works personally selected by Georgia O'Keeffe.

Cities Everywhere Sell Dreams

Jazz was born in New Orleans, and the King Bolden Band (top, before 1895) may well have been the first group to push it through a horn. If so, then Buddy Bolden (back row to the right of the string bass) could well be the "inventor" of this American musical phenomenon. A mixture of improvisation and uptown rag, it leveled adoring audiences. The King was committed to the state hospital in 1907 after living too fast and playing too hard. By 1904 in Washington, young Edward Kennedy Ellington, right, was ready to take up the piano. The Duke developed into one of America's greatest composers. Opposite, Madeleine MacQuigau—evidently a violinist of Victorian times—made no lasting impact on music, but her dreamy carte-de-visite is a classic of its kind.

Cities Inspire Fashions of the Times

As the 20th century arrived in triumph, mothers and daughters of America's rising middle class discovered independence, self-confidence, and up-to-the minute fashions designed and manufactured in the cities. Top, beads and bows of 1911 set off the bright faces of three young women, the eldest named Eleanor Custis. Left, Florence Evelyn Nesbit, captured in 1902 by the camera of Rudolf Eickemeyer, Jr., posed for the original Gibson Girl drawing and became America's first great fashion model. Women celebrated her adventurous spirit and glamour. Later enmeshed in scandal, she was known as "the girl in the red velvet swing." (See also pages 12 and 13.) Opposite, from 1929, a bride in South Bend, Indiana, makes a fashion statement in a gown that incorporates both traditional and modern elements—"Something old, something new."

A Capitol Arises In The Capital City

As the nation grew, so did the Capitol building. A massive facelift, begun in 1851 on July 4th, added the present day House and Senate wings, and a new dome. Secretary of War Jefferson Davis appointed army engineer Montgomery Meigs, right, as superintendent in 1853.

Work on the dome continued throughout the Civil War as a symbol of the Union.

To See: To Be Seen

Yankton Sioux delegation visits the Capitol in horseless carriages, 1905, left. Native dress is rare in this period as tribal delegates usually wanted to dress like whites. Top, riding a new and untippable bike, a member of the American Wheelman organization pits his skill against the Capitol steps.

It's a complex fate, being an American. . . .
— Henry James

184

AT HOME IN THE HINTERLANDS

Thomas Jefferson, who was said to represent more brain power dining alone than all the other presidents at a banquet, believed that it would take forty generations to settle the great continental vastness of America. As it turned out, scarcely four generations passed between the explorations of Lewis and Clark, commissioned by Jefferson in 1803, and the presumed closing of the frontier in 1893.

The settlers just walked right in, sat right down, and made themselves at home. How could it happen so fast?

There are plenty of good reasons, but surely the most important impulse to settle the nation's interior derived from the sheer availability of land. The New World played host to a real-estate revelation. For the first time in human memory, an ordinary family could actually own the land—it belonged to no emperor, king, caliph, or lord. And they could realize the wealth of the land for themselves, its minerals and timber and crops. "It is not too soon," Jefferson wrote to a friend when the future president was ambassador to France, "to

provide by every possible means that as few as possible shall be without a little portion of land."

But it was one thing to own it and quite another to farm it. In this regard, those who believe that the most significant technological event affecting the history of America is the aeroplane, or the incandescent bulb, or the computer chip, are wrong. They have forgotten about the mass-produced steel moldboard plow, developed in 1839 by John Deere, a blacksmith originally from Rutland, Vermont, who set up his small factory on the Illinois prairie.

The plow was light, strong, and inexpensive, and it would last. With a Deere plow, or one of its later imitators, a farmer—any farmer—could zip open prairie sod that had been unyielding with the old-fashioned iron-clad wooden plows it now replaced. This was the key to the resistant plains, the billion-acre central third of the continent. Now, finally, the nation could decisively break away from a coast-bound colonial period that had lasted nearly two centuries. In *Pioneer Women*, Joanna Stratton's remarkable collection of contemporary accounts of settling the Kansas prairie a hundred years ago, Mrs. J. H. O'Loughlin describes how the virgin sod was turned, in strips two feet wide, with a single-bottom plow and a team of oxen. After that, she says, "We . . . used an ax or hatchet to make a hole in the

---

In the Dakotas (*c.* 1900), far from doctors, a mother buys nostrums from the trader, top. Spunky young woman's close cut, opposite, may have begun with a shaved head—home remedy for contagious ringworm and nits.

sod, then dropped the seed and closed the hole with our heels."

And so was the great heartland settled, by steel, an acre at a time. The continent was ours. The Homestead Act, signed by President Lincoln in 1862, at last provided the "little portion" that Jefferson had sought. With that act, the ownership of 147 million acres, in 160-acre parcels, was transferred from the federal government to some 1.6 million families like the O'Loughlins of Kansas. They constructed their "soddies," houses made of turves of prairie grass; they collected buffalo chips for fuel; and they created a skein of rural villages across the land. Writing in the bicentennial issue of *Smithsonian* (July 1976), British economist Norman Macrae describes the homesteaders' achievement as "just about the most decent, as well as progressive, small-town neighborhood system the world has seen."

It is true that not all Americans shared equally in the bounty of land, and some of the small towns were more decent than others. The home in the hinterlands has often been a cruel one, for Indians confined to desolate reservations, Blacks who started out on the cotton fields as slaves and would end up as slave-wage sharecroppers, poor whites whose plowed-out soil on the southern plains turned to dust, Japanese-Americans interned during World War II, Chicano fruit pickers whose hands now shake involuntarily from pesticide poisoning.

And yet, despite these reminders of a sometimes-grim reality, the hinterlands remain the locus of the essential American dream—the Jeffersonian ideal of a life of dignity and sufficiency on the land as a matter of *right*, of a small-town rural society expressive of the best in the American character. It really happened and, it would seem, it happened only yesterday.

Charles E. Little

In 1909, 34 men and 50 horses of the Canadian-American Alaska Boundary Survey slog through summer mud, below, to settle a boundary dispute between their two countries. Though the United States had purchased Alaska from Russia in 1867, exact border demarcations had not been a major problem until 30,000 Americans descended upon the Yukon during the Klondike gold rush of 1896. Thriving on the rugged life, people thronged into the Far North. Some brought their own gear, but others outfitted at places such as Sheep Camp, Alaska, left.

ke heavy going.

Restless Americans moved not only themselves but even their houses about the landscape, opposite. The feat, by wheel or water, amazed European observers. The New World Noah who launched his duplex ark from Pittsburgh probably left the furniture inside. Moving of conventional housing is still done, though mobile homes have raised the idea to a high level of sophistication.

Before the railroads, thousands of miles of canals and rivers served as the nation's primary economic lifelines: varied craft carried manufactured goods as well as commodities. George Washington was the father of the Chesapeake and Ohio Canal, above. Its barges of coal traveled the 185 miles from Cumberland, Maryland, to Washington, D.C., and thence to the Chesapeake Bay. Above at right,

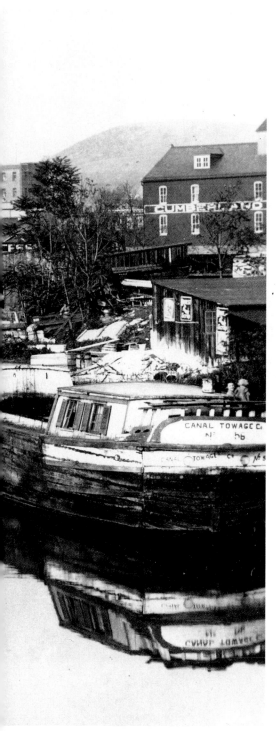

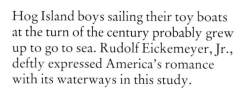

Hog Island boys sailing their toy boats at the turn of the century probably grew up to go to sea. Rudolf Eickemeyer, Jr., deftly expressed America's romance with its waterways in this study.

College women collect marine specimens, left, at Woods Hole, Massachusetts, site of the famed Marine Biology Laboratory. From its opening in 1888, Woods Hole accepted all qualified scholars, a policy that encouraged scientific education for women of means. Custom and economics, though, decreed that poor kids work: Lewis Hine's 1912 photograph reveals the lot of child oyster shuckers, top. Standing all day, enduring painful shell cuts and infection, they were paid a nickel for each pail they filled; the best workers earned only a dime a day. Men continued to handle commercial fishing as exemplified by a halibut catch from the Grand Banks, above.

Neither Snow Nor Rain...

Bringing city to country and knitting the nation together, the Postal Service first established routes to remote areas in 1896 when the program called Rural Free Delivery was inaugurated. In 1916, 42,000 rural carriers served small towns such as the one above. Virtually all the country is covered by RFD by 1931, when the Texas farmer, opposite, reads his agricultural magazine. The mailman is still a welcomed and revered part of home towns everywhere, as below in Utah's San Juan County at Blanding in the early 1900s.

The Billion-Acre Heartland

Cyrus McCormick's introduction of the horse-drawn reaper in 1831 forever changed the face of American agriculture. No longer were farmers reduced to the back-breaking harvest labor of the cradle scythe, shown at top in a re-enactment. Toward the end of the century, McCormick's reaper and Jerome Case's threshing technologies were integrated into huge combines, right. Big rigs and herds of horses were required to harvest vast acreage in the plains of the Midwest and Northwest. Even after mechanization, some crops still required hand labor, as in apple orchards of Virginia's Shenandoah Valley during 1910.

196

Marketing acumen made H.J. Heinz much more than a "pickle king," despite the words on the wagon, top, *c.* 1900. His entrepreneurial daring catapulted the little-known tomato into most households. He also produced far more than his modern-day slogan's "57 Varieties" and developed a special tomato that tastes exactly like his ketchup. Far left, Heinz tomatoes are washed and sorted before processing. Left, about 1900, orange tree cuttings are stored in an "insectory" to propagate ladybugs, a biological weapon in the fight against scale infection of citrus crops.

King Cotton held court in postbellum Dixie towns on auction day, as above right. The real cotton kingdom, though, was the field. In the South after the Civil War, a white manager, above left, weighs the cotton picked by black workers. Emancipation did not free Blacks from onerous working conditions: share-cropping was simply substituted for slavery. Under this system, the 'cropper paid the landowner half his harvest,

from which the landowner deducted usurious interest on loans for food, clothing, and other necessities. No money was left over, only bondage. And Ol' Man River still brought the steamboats to carry the cotton away. In fact, easy transport on several remarkable southern river systems helped keep the antebellum plantation system intact well into the twentieth century. Damage to the soil and the invasion of the boll weevil finally broke King Cotton's absolute sway.

Tobacco Road runs right inside the 1939 North Carolina farmhouse of Titus Oakley and family. Using their bedroom as a barn, the entire family strips, ties, and grades big tobacco leaves. Few tobacco farmers complained about the conditions, however, because this cash crop kept them solvent during the depression-ridden 1930s. Top, a Pennsylvania Dutch farmer and his daughter cut tobacco in Lancaster County. The industry has always been responsive to the blandishments of the adman, attested, above, by tobacco-leaf-clad promoters in the 1950s.

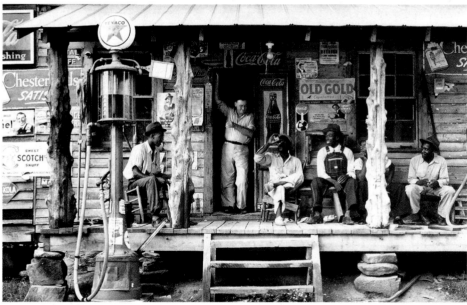

From Field to Factory

By 1910, Blacks owned a quarter of a million farms in the Deep South: today, fewer than 50,000. With the crash of 1929, a vast migration began, lasting more than a decade. Right, a Florida family heads for New Jersey in 1940. But another factor also came into play. Even as a rural Black culture arose after the Civil War, a particularly strident form of racism emerged to oppose it. Lynching and burnings were rare but legalized prejudice flourished, as with a colored-only water cooler in Oklahoma, top. Tobacco Road, above, had its special brand of white paternalism.

Rough justice, company-style affected strikers. The incident at right occurred in West Virginia during a strike in 1932 at the Mountaineer Coal Company. At the time, union leaders were organizing economically depressed Appalachia. "Breaker boys," top, spent 12-hour shifts picking slate from coal moving past on conveyor belts. Shetland ponies often lived and died in the pits pulling coal carts.

206

In the American hinterlands, isolation and privation gave rise to an intense form of religious piety, evoked at left with sensitivity by Rudolf Eickemeyer, Jr., in his study of a man and his Bible. H.L. Mencken described small southern towns as being part of the "Bible Belt." Such a town appears in 1940 at Christmastime, opposite: Gadsden, Alabama. Though Mencken used his term scornfully, southern fundamentalists have always been proud of their religious heritage. They have instilled it into their children as "hot gospel" at tent meetings or more quietly at home in prayer, as shown in the sentimental 1906 image of a young girl praying, above.

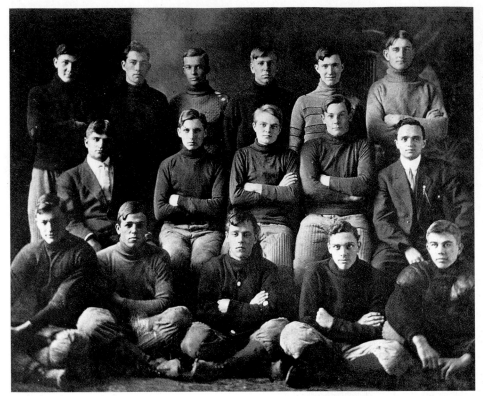

If a log-cabin birth personified the ideal of a 19th-century president, then the ideal cradle of leadership for most of the 20th century has been the small town. In the hinterlands, a boy could learn manly values through military training. Young Christian men ride with the 5th "Calvary" in Texas, opposite, or compete in sports. Dwight D. "Ike" Eisenhower excelled as a player on his Abilene, Kansas, football team, above (third from left in top row). But Ike's small-town friendliness and persistence—more than his athletic skill—won the collective heart of the nation.

COPYRIGHTED BY CHAS. THOMPSON. WEIGHT 30,000 L
PHOTO. BY HANDGO. MIAMI. FLORIDA. 1913.

LENGTH 45, FT.

Whopper!

For sheer exuberance, nothing will ever beat the American hinterlands. Thirty-thousand pounds of whale shark trucks through the streets of a small town with big ambitions—Miami, Florida. The saga of the big fish that did not get away was celebrated in 1913.

The country town is one of the great American institutions; perhaps the greatest . . . in shaping public sentiment and giving character to American culture.
—Thorstein Veblen

211

PART FOUR

TAKING OUR SHOW ON THE ROAD

Timothy Foote

At dawn on May 1, 1898, Commodore George Dewey's nine modern warships steamed into Manila Bay and opened fire on ten antique Spanish vessels anchored there. When the shooting stopped, almost nothing was left of Spain's fleet. In six hours, at a cost of only eight wounded American sailors, the United States of America had become a world power.

Americans were bursting with energy just then and raring to spread the gospel of democracy and free enterprise beyond our shores. In this sadder, and perhaps wiser, post-Vietnam era, the rush of rhetoric that burst forth after Dewey's victory can scarcely be believed. Acclaimed almost hysterically, the commodore became a national hero overnight; his command, "You may fire when ready, Gridley," entered the language. There were Dewey dolls and special medals and plans to run him for president. As one U.S. senator put it, "Americans are trustees of the world's progress, guardians of its righteous peace." Charles Denby, a member of President McKinley's commission on the Philippines—which we had just liberated from the Spanish yoke—spoke for many of his countrymen when he declared: "We are taking our proper rank among the nations of the world. We are after markets, the greatest markets now existing in the world. Along with these markets will go our beneficent institutions; and humanity will bless us."

But, when we voted to annex the Philippines, those Filipino rebels who had been struggling for their independence after more than three hundred years of Spanish rule found themselves obliged to fight their American liberators. A cruel guerrilla war left twenty thousand people dead, most of them Filipino. The once isolated, and isolationist, United States swiftly discovered that being a world power can be a painful, perplexing, and mostly thankless proposition.

This was unsettling news. Yet, in taking our show on the road during the next half century or so, we proved overwhelmingly successful in trade and war and the exportation of what we took to be good works. American confidence ran high. And as if it needed further bolstering, records of all sorts fell to a succession of Americans, from channel swimmer Gertrude Ederle to sprinter Jesse Owens, but most dramatically in the conquest of the air. Probably the most authentically Yankee hero abroad ever was Wilbur Wright, breaking records and making sales with the Wright Flyer in 1908. Wearing a plain cloth cap, doing his own work on the aircraft, unimpressed by the rich and famous who flocked to see him, Wright became one of the first great celebrities of the twentieth century as "the ideal American." Frenchmen even copied his headwear, creating a fashion fad for a slouch chapeau calling itself the "Veelber Reet."

America came back in 1917. With little or nothing to fear from Germany, and little to gain except helping preserve parliamentary democracy in Europe, the United States threw its hat in the ring "over there," turned the tide of battle for the exhausted combatants and left 120,000 Americans dead in places like Chateau-Thierry, Belleau Wood, and the Argonne. Hardly more than twenty years later, as if playing the second act of a Greek tragedy, it had to be done all over again, in World War II, this time on a global scale, this time with freedom and democracy truly in jeopardy. After that war, when we had helped establish the United Nations and

Preceding pages: In 1888, old salts swap stories aboard the USS *Mohican*. They link the old, all-wood navy to the new iron fleet. These pages: Faces of Al and Ruth Wilson shine with optimism and adventure at the National Air Races of 1928 in Los Angeles.

created the Marshall Plan to help finance the revival of fallen foe and friend alike, Henry Luce's declaration that the twentieth century would be "the American Century" did not seem overblown at all.

Every American who lived through World War II, though, heard the celebrated English complaint about American soldiers in Britain, who were, it was said, "oversexed, overpaid and over here." Such Old World attitudes—and they came in many forms—did not rapidly improve, either. Americans sometimes wonder why their "road show" both attracts and irritates the rest of the world.

"America," F. Scott Fitzgerald once wrote, "is a willingness of the heart." If that is not quite as true now as it once was, at least where overseas efforts are concerned, it may be because the one thing that, at our best, we wanted to share with the world is something that does not travel. That is simply what, at our best, we *are* here at home: still a remarkably classless, remarkably free, remarkably stable land full-to-overflowing with opportunity. Henry Luce's idea of an "American Century," and the extreme dream of beneficent world influence that blossomed after Dewey's victory at Manila Bay, both probably shut down for good when Saigon fell to the North Vietnamese in 1975. But the streams of immigrants from all over the world keep coming, proof that what we have to offer is still unique.

Though it sometimes does not seem so, the Old World has not entirely forgotten our willingness of the heart. I visited Chateau-Thierry once, trying to do an interview piece about local reaction to a French national crisis. Chateau-Thierry was then a communist-dominated workers' town, I knew, walls speckled with anti-American slogans. But it bore a name that American readers might respond to.

To get any cooperation at all, I was told, I needed the help of the owner of the *Tout Va Bien Café*, who turned out to be a vast, grim gorgon of a woman, slouched over the cash register (where else?), with a *Gaulois* drooping from the corner of her mouth. While I explained what I wanted in my best Anglo-Saxon French, all the patrons of the place listened in attentive silence, like the denizens of those bars in movie westerns waiting for the tenderfoot to speak his piece and then be tossed out. There was a pregnant pause. Then Madame growled her approval.

"Why not," she said. "There are not a few American friends up there on the hill." And she jerked her head in the direction of the World War I cemetery above town, where, on a broad expanse of well-kept lawn, legions of white crosses permanently stand at parade rest.

TWENTIETH CENTURY UNLIMITED

ontague Roberts has good reason to beam. His driving team and their 60-horsepower Thomas Flyer have just won the New York-to-Paris auto race of 1908, billed as the longest ever. And long it is—around the world chasing the sun, 22,000 miles of bad roads, and no roads at all.

The victory is perhaps the high-water mark for the E.R. Thomas Motor Company of Buffalo, New York. The company has sold 700 of its 1907 four-cylinder Flyers at $4,000 apiece, a pretty penny in a day when you can build a nine-room house for little more than half as much. But a tidal wave is coming that will sweep away almost all of the hundreds of little auto companies like E.R. Thomas. 1908 is the year that Henry Ford will introduce the Model T.

By 1926, when the Model T is discontinued, Ford will have sold more than 15 million of the go-anywhere "flivvers" to a public made car-crazy by their very availability. Ford has realized that if you aim for the broad market, you can sell enough to keep the price down where most folks can afford it. He will sell some Model Ts for as little as $290.

Nor, of course, is Ford alone. Nearly everyone has heard the message. While smoke-belching mills still stamp out the beams and trusses for bridges and skyscrapers, a new, lighter beat is echoing through the halls of U.S. commerce. It is the sound of a new kind of industry for a new kind of customer: the consumer. Born of advertising, merchandising, and ever-fatter paychecks, the consumer industry is already making electric fans, toasters, vacuum cleaners, and other helpful household gadgets. Soon, the trickle of consumer items will become a flood, a torrent of can't-live-without-'em products that will dominate the U.S. economy.

Meanwhile, just over the horizon, a galaxy of services will spring up to take care of the ever-more-mobile population, while new technologies and materials bring unimaginable changes to every facet of life.

But by then, several wars older and wiser, the U.S. will have reached a kind of maturity, as the place where the consumer society evolved and grew before it spread all over the world. It'll be very different then than it is now, in 1908, just before we put the show on the road.

Drivers Montague Roberts, opposite, and George Schuster, above (behind wheel), circle the globe during 1908 to win an international automobile race in the Thomas Flyer.

Alexis Doster III

Armed and armor-clad as St. Joan of Arc, a World War I recruiter, above, reflects the optimism of America in 1917. Congress and the president had rallied the nation to the Allied cause. Perhaps most celebrated of all World War I American war heroes was air ace Eddie Rickenbacker, upper right, who shot down 26 German planes. One year after it declared war on Germany in April 1917, the United States was well on the way to becoming a mighty arsenal. Women also played their part to keep factories running as does this driver of an electrical truck that moves a turbine, far right.

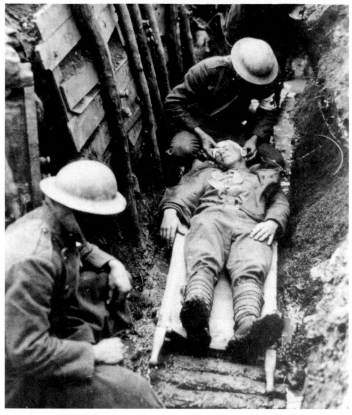

The Yanks Are Coming

American soldiers come to the relief of war-torn France in November 1918, right, with doughboys like Philip Tangor (left) and Allen Floyd, welcomed by Mr. and Mrs. Baloux of the Ardennes. Bloody trench fighting claimed a quarter of a million American casualties, including the marine on a stretcher, top. Above, an infantry squad assembles in full field dress. One of every four fighting men was either killed or wounded during the 18 months of American involvement.

Life on the Edge

Swooping close to the waters of San Francisco Bay during January 1911, daring test pilot Eugene Ely launches his Curtiss biplane from the decks of the U.S.S. *Pennsylvania*, left, where he had landed an hour earlier. His pioneering efforts rely on new arresting devices similar to the hook-and-cable system that today's U.S. Navy uses to snag planes during carrier landings. Tough competence marks the stance of another aviation pioneer, William "Big Bill" Hopson, above. As an airmail pilot during the 1920s, he braved foul weather and darkness in an era before airfield lights and other safety features. He crashed and died before the decade ended.

Coast to Coast

Both airport and railroad station, Ohio's Port Columbus, opposite, served as a transfer point for the nation's first transcontinental air-rail service in 1929. Flying by day and snoozing by night in a Pullman berth, a passenger could ride the very expensive "Lindbergh Line" from New York to Los Angeles in the fastest time possible—48 hours. Right, the Golden Gate Bridge spans the mile-wide entrance to San Francisco Bay. It is an engineering, organizational, and financial accomplishment of the highest order. Engineers planted deep, earthquake-resistant foundations upon which the 4,200-foot suspension bridge would stand. Top, two workers adjust cables "up top" before the mighty span's 1937 completion. Their perch can be seen in the scenic view.

An Invisible Empire

Opposite, pioneer amateur radio enthusiast Nathan Pomerantz used his short-wave radio to communicate with other radio "hams" around the world. Millions enjoy his hobby today. Most Americans, though, were content to tune in to their local radio station and just listen. Above, an Inuit family pays rapt attention to a 1926 broadcast from a large Zenith set. Almost overnight, the radio became a household fixture as young women, right, and millions of other Americans tuned in to a steady diet of news, entertainment, fashion, sports, and advertisements.

227

1. Paul Robeson

2. Gloria Swanson

5. Pearl S. Buck

6. Edna St. Vincent Millay

3. Sinclar Lewis

4. Eugene O'Neill

The early-to-mid nineteenth century witnessed a profusion of American talent in the arts, including the following individuals with portraits in the collections of the Smithsonian's National Portrait Gallery:

1. **Paul Robeson** (1898-1976): singer, actor, and political activist.

2. **Gloria Swanson** (1899-1983): stage and screen actress.

3. **Sinclair Lewis** (1885-1951): novelist and social critic, the first American to win the Nobel Prize in literature.

4. **Eugene O'Neill** (1888-1953): Pulitzer- and Nobel-Prize-winning playwright.

5. **Pearl S. Buck** (1892-1973): Pulitzer- and Nobel-Prize-winning author.

6. **Edna St. Vincent Millay** (1892-1950): Pulitzer-Prize-winning poet.

7. **Ernest Hemingway** (1899-1961): Nobel-Prize-winning novelist.

8. **Cecil B. DeMille** (1881-1959): film producer, noted for spectacles and epics with casts of thousands.

7. Ernest Hemingway and his son, John

8. Cecil B. DeMille

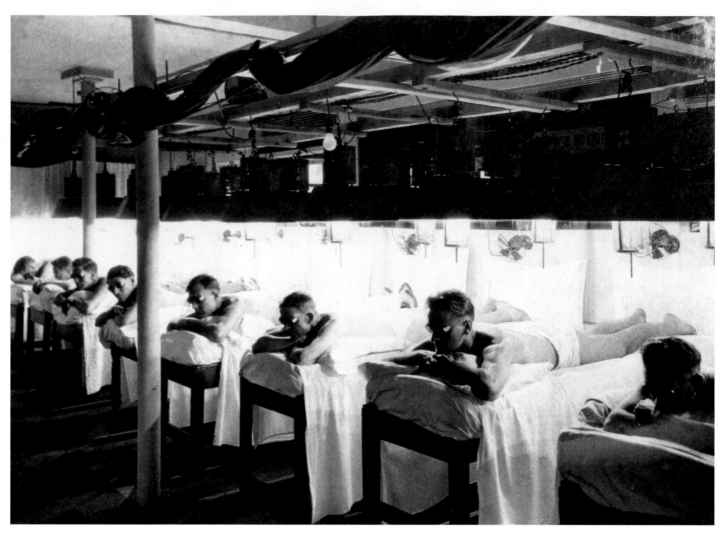

People and Technology

California medical student John Larson invented the polygraph, or "lie detector," tested on Ruth Hillman by Ruth Richman, opposite. Above, patients receive sunlamp therapy at a sanitarium in Battle Creek, Michigan. Years earlier at the same site, young W.K. Kellogg worked for his brother, studied nutrition and, in 1906, started his breakfast food company. Right, the "King of Corn Flakes" appears in his cereal factory. Working quietly through a foundation, Mr. Kellogg turned his huge profits into health and education programs for children. He became one of America's great humanitarians.

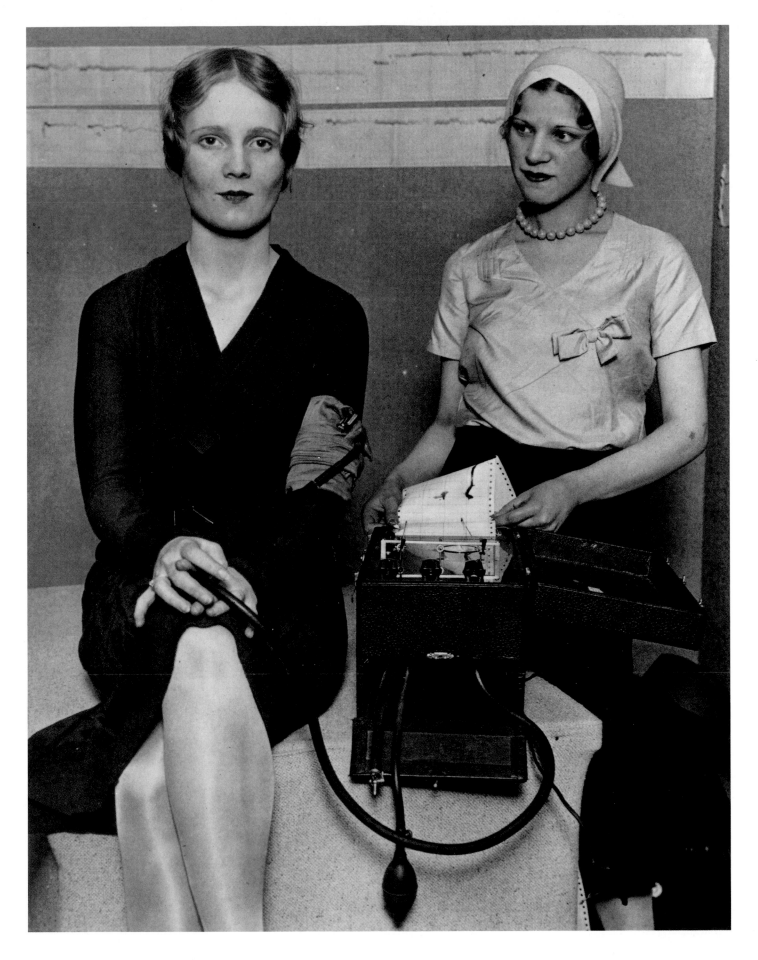

A Sleeping Giant Awakens

Destroyer *Shaw* explodes at its dry dock, top, during the Japanese air attack on Pearl Harbor. Galvanized into action, the nation responded with an immense industrial mobilization. Opposite, production "soldiers" complete their shift at the Homestead Steel Works in Munhall, Pennsylvania, where 50 tons of hot steel is forged into a turbine rotor shaft, above. Left, workers pour molten steel into molds at Columbia Steel Company's California plant.

Above left, chin set, a victim of wartime hysteria after Pearl Harbor asserts his human dignity. Of Japanese heritage, he and his grandsons have been arrested and await transportation to a relocation center during World War II. Fears of wartime treachery on the part of U.S. citizens of Japanese descent proved groundless. More than 100,000 American citizens of Japanese ancestry were sent into internal exile in remote camps such as California's Manzanar, opposite. Ironically, while the camps were filled, many young Americans of Japanese descent fought for the Allied cause overseas, as at top. Daniel Inouye, above at right, now a United States senator, served with the 442nd Regimental Combat Team, a group that earned more than 18,000 individual decorations for bravery.

An all-woman team, left, puts finishing touches on the plexiglass noses of A-20 Havoc light bombers at a Douglas Aircraft plant at Long Beach, California. Almost a third of the millions of women working in 1944 were formerly full-time homemakers. At the Imperial Works plant in Oil City, Pennsylvania, above, women examine 37-millimeter projectiles during a 28-point inspection process. Top, ball turret gunner W. E. Cosby of Bardwell, Kentucky, prepares to deliver the goods.

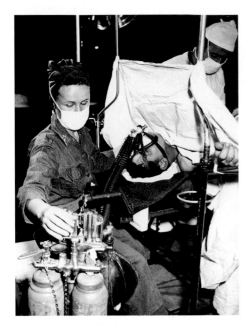

In Korea, off-duty surgeons of the 8055th Mobile Army Surgical Hospital (MASH) sip champagne. They and all their fellow nurses and medical support personnel across Korea helped inspire the popular book, motion picture, and television series. In its first 16 months, the 8055th moved 27 times. Such mobility and the use of helicopters enabled MASH units to provide full surgical services just minutes from the front. More than 95 percent of the patients treated at Korean MASH units survived, including the man anesthetized, top, by a nurse at the 44th MASH. Above, at the 1st MASH, diners line up to dunk their metal mess kits in big cans of boiling soapy water. Followed by a clear rinse, this was dishwashing front-line style.

Into a New Era

With an expansive wave of the hat, Harry S Truman moves from the presidency into private life. With his wife, Bess, the ex-president departs Washington, D.C., for Independence, Missouri, in January 1953. Plenty of old-fashioned grit and grin marked "give-'em-hell-Harry's" seven turbulent years in office. His time saw the end of World War II—history's hottest—and the beginning of a chilling interlude between the U.S. and the U.S.S.R. Marilyn Monroe, top—a sizzling film goddess of the Cold War era—greets American service people in Japan at the close of the Korean War.

KEEP THE FEELING ALIVE

Jim Wallace

O ur best photographs convey much more than simple fact; they can communicate a feeling for people and the times that they inhabited. Properly cared for, both the pictures and the feeling can be kept alive. This need not be only a backward-looking pursuit, though. Photographs of ourselves will be the window on today for those in the future.

Consider that the people who will most appreciate today's family photographs have probably not yet been born. They'll be the ones many years hence who get a lump in the

Left, Mathew Brady portrait of Nelly and Jesse, children of U.S. Grant. Top, early tour group at U.S. Capital.

throat looking at photographs of their grandparents or great grandparents. And there's a special thrill seeing one's own parents as a young couple, or oneself as a child, or one's own children just a few years earlier.

Your descendants may be interested in the fact, for instance, that you traveled to Yellowstone, Cape Kennedy, Hawaii, or the national capital. Maybe you attended a presidential inauguration, or even gathered with others on the Mall in Washington, D.C., to hear the prophetic "I Have a Dream" speech of Reverend Martin Luther King, Jr., on August 28, 1963. Perhaps you quietly, privately, searched for the name of a son or daughter carved in the granite of the Vietnam War Memorial.

Many such experiences, from trips or from the neighborhood, are frozen in your photographs, never to change, and ready to tell those who follow exactly what it looked like—if we save it for them. Unfortunately, that can be a big "if." All too often, family history goes into the trash and is gone forever. Throwing away your family photographs is actually blinding history. Many of the photographs on the preceding pages could easily have been lost. Few of the photographers who took them would ever have dreamed their work would be part of a book such as this. Yet these pages of faces and events from the past were preserved. And as a result we have all learned and benefited.

All too often we assume that only

Bits and pieces: upper left, Amelia C. Van Buren and her cat *c.* 1891 (Eakins); far left, man in mirrors; left, inventor with his drying rack; above, Smithsonian Castle late 1800s; upper right, Reese family of Accident, Maryland (1892); right, Lela Jenkins of Talladega, Alabama; far right, corporal of artillery U.S.A.; farthest right, Alliene Jenkins (left) and Lela Jenkins, both of Talladega.

local and state historical societies— or a major museum complex such as the Smithsonian—are prepared to keep old photographs. Certainly, they have their place. But they can't keep everything, nor should they.

Local history is most important locally, and family history is most important to the immediate family. And that's where to begin. The primary rule is, never throw old family photographs away. Second, take care of your photos—old or new.

Albums are especially valuable. More than just a group of miscella-neous photographs, they tell a story and have context. The images they contain have been edited with a purpose. They were seen as the most important at the time. The people who took them wanted to show them off. Portraying a relatively small group over a specific period of time, the album is a visual diary. There's nothing else quite like it.

Albums should be kept together if at all possible. Passed from generation to generation, their value increases with age. So do the problems of preserving them. Most albums, including those available today, are simply not archival. They may con-tain paper with a high acid content as well as a variety of glues and adhesives, all of which deteriorate with age. Unfortunately, as they perish, albums damage the photographs they contain.

If you examine an old album and find the pages badly yellowed, turning brittle and perhaps showing an outline of a photograph traced on the facing page, it's clear there are problems. Archival quality, acid-free albums are becoming increasingly available. They are like an insurance policy for the preservation of your pictures. This is especially important if the album is already a generation or more old. Carefully transfer pictures from old albums to new, keeping them in the same order and

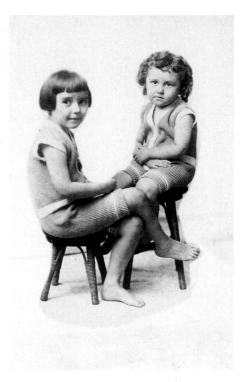

Liart. Military Corporal.

position and use archival quality fasteners. Information is readily available from the makers of such products.

Also keep the same kinds of archival materials in mind as you put current photographs in albums. It's generally easier to obtain the proper materials and use them the first time. And remember to write on the back of the print the date and the names of the people and places pictured. It is sometimes assumed that because a set of prints exists, the negatives are no longer needed. Quite the opposite is true. Some of the most tragic photographic losses occur when the original negatives are discarded. If anything, the negatives are more important than the prints. With them more prints can be made, and they are often easier to keep.

Special problems arise if you have many negatives but few prints; these hints may help. Handle negatives as little as possible. Cotton knit gloves, from the same sources as above, can protect both prints and negatives. "Reading" photographic negatives is difficult and to save handling you may find it useful to copy negatives onto 35mm film. To do this, backlight the negatives. Sunlight reflected against the back of a pane of flat, frosted glass can provide good illumination. But, first, seek the advice of a professional photographer in evaluating your particular needs.

In the future, though, electronics may come to your rescue. Already there are some video-based devices with which negatives can be viewed as positive images on a television screen. This aids in editing and sorting. One day, camcorders may possess features that allow you to change a negative to a positive image at the push of a button. More on the video revolution later.

Organizing your photographic collection highlights the value of each item and also makes research easier and more effective. Family members, each with special knowledge of various relatives, can work together to illuminate their common heritage as represented in the photographs. In many cases, individuals will discover images they had never seen, or had forgotten, and they will want copies of them. Where the negatives no longer exist, copy negatives can be made. When important original prints have begun to deteriorate, copy negatives should be made anyway.

Above all, store your photographic prints in a cool, dry area. For black-and-white, separate "sick" prints from healthy ones. Segregate prints mounted on cardboard or other backing—which may contain acid—from unmounted

photographic prints on paper.

Proper storage is especially important with color. During the last generation, we have turned almost completely towards color. The results are certainly more lifelike, but unfortunately the photographs deteriorate more easily than black-and-white. You may not know that many professional photographers can sometimes copy prints or slides whose colors have changed, in some cases improving hues through the use of filters.

As with fabrics and other materials containing dyes, color photographs will fade if subjected to light over a long period of time. But color photographs can also fade, even in total darkness, from the effects of heat and humidity. Black-and-white photographs can become spotted be-

cause of air pollution. Keeping photographs locked up in the attic or basement is certainly not the answer.

Under ideal conditions, the original negatives or color transparencies should be kept as cool as possible, even below freezing, and at a relative humidity below 50 percent but no lower than 15 percent. Ordinary refrigerators will do more harm than good because the relative humidity inside a standard refrigerator is extremely high. Cold air cannot hold as much moisture as warm air, so the *relative* humidity of the same air is much higher at 35 degrees than at 50 degrees.

Many institutions, such as the Smithsonian, which specialize in storing photographs, have built specially designed cold rooms for this purpose. This usually isn't practical

for individuals, no matter how good a family's intentions. There is an alternative, however. Put the negatives and transparencies into an airtight bag or series of bags. Squeeze out as much of the inside air as possible, seal the bag, and then place it in a refrigerator or freezer. This may seem like a major commitment, but the photographs of a family reunion or a child's first birthday party can never be replaced. And if the house burns down the refrigerator or freezer may make a good fire-resistant safe.

If the time ever comes when the family cannot keep a collection of photographs, alternatives should be sought rather than throwing them away. A photographic collection's main benefit is to the local area where it was created. So keep prints and negatives you can no longer care for close to home. State and local history associations and libraries can help, and at several levels.

Unidentified dancers, cyclists, far left; Vietnam Memorial viewers (1980s), left; 1933 swearing-in of Franklin D. Roosevelt, possibly the first color picture of a presidential inauguration, above; right, first presidential inauguration to be photographed with a still, color electronic camera—of George Bush, 1989.

First, libraries and history associations provide information about sorting, storing, and maintaining photographs. They can also serve as a repository for photographs of local or regional significance, such as a collection of family photographs that document the community and its residents during a specific period of time.

In addition, local libraries and associations should consider installing equipment to help local residents make copy negatives. A copy stand need not be elaborate, but with set lighting and exposure maintained, patrons can supply their own film to make copies of prized prints.

As a lesser alternative, the current generation of electrostatic copying machines makes marginally acceptable reference prints. They will be fine to send to distant relatives who may want copies of some of your prints. At an office supply store you may be able to buy a cheap "dot-pattern screen," which will help you make clear reproductions on the electrostatic copier.

For storing and sending lots of prints, investigate the use of a camcorder to create a video cassette. Commercial copying of prints onto a video costs only a few dollars at some city department stores, or you may be able to do it yourself. In any case, putting your negatives, prints, and even slide shows on video is an increasingly attractive and practical alternative to handling, and perhaps damaging, valuable photos. Through the VCR, you can see family history on TV. And as libraries embrace digital and other computer-based solutions for information retrieval, such facilities can play a major role in helping to document and preserve local visual history.

Today, thanks to 150 years of photographic experience, we have truly become a visual society, with new technologies accelerating the trend. In the future we will continue to take and save family photographs, but the album of tomorrow could be vastly different.

During the last few years an entirely new generation of cameras has been introduced. Automatic focus and exposure, combined with built-in flash and zoom lenses, all controlled by internal computer chips, make the new cameras almost impossible to fool.

Today, electronic cameras are poised to enter the consumer market-place. These cameras use small magnetic disks in place of film. As with a camcorder, their pictures require no developing, no waiting. They can be viewed at once on a television set and then printed almost instantly. No matter what sort of equipment we use, we should remember that how we take the photograph is not nearly as important as the images we capture. Great events, even in the course of world history, can pale compared to the birth of a new grandchild. Our own personal "great events" occur regularly each year, and the photographs we take and save are of more importance to us than a Pulitzer Prize-winner.

In those photographs we hold America's real history in our hands. They are not only worth caring for—conserving and preserving—they are worth caring about, just as the next generation, and those to follow, are worth caring about.

AUTHORS

Roger Bruns, who wrote captions for "Lincoln—A Singular Vision," is the Deputy Executive Director of the National Historical Publications and Records Commission at the National Archives. Author of several books including *Knights of the Road: A Hobo History*, and *The Damndest Radical*, he also has written numerous articles and several biographies.

Tom D. Crouch, the author of "The Promised Land," is a historian of aviation, and cultural and community life. He chairs the Department of Social and Cultural History at the Smithsonian's National Museum of American History. Here he recently directed a permanent exhibit on the internment of Americans of Japanese heritage during World War II. The author of numerous books on the history of flight, his most recent is *The Bishop's Boys: A Life of Wilbur and Orville Wright*.

Timothy Foote, a Senior Editor at *Smithsonian* magazine, authored "Taking Our Show on the Road." He often writes about history and culture. *Smithsonian* articles include, "Imagining a Constitutionless past," and "After more than two centuries, this may be Mr. Madison's year." He was also a foreign correspondent for *Time-Life* in Paris. Mr. Foote was an advisor for *Images*.

John Hoke provided his reminiscences of growing up during the 1930s in "Little Ol' New York et al." He has been Biological Engineering Specialist at the United States Park Service since 1970, is the author several books, and has written for *Smithsonian* and other magazines. He served as a photographic advisor for the *Images of America* book project, especially Part Three, and contributed the photographic "Kim's Game" on page 141.

Mary M. Ison wrote "How We Like to See Ourselves." She joined the photo collections staff of the Library of Congress in 1974 and is currently Head of Photos at the Office of Prints and Photographs. Her recent research includes analysis of snapshots of Uriah Hunt Painter, an early 20th-century photographer. Mary Ison also provided early advice for this book project.

Charles E. Little, author of text and the captions for "At Home in the Hinterlands," as well as captions for "Moving on West," is a Washington-based writer on natural resources and the environment. His credits include *Challenge of the Land*, and *Green Fields Forever* and he published previously with Smithsonian Books in *The American Land*.

Diane Vogt O'Connor, who wrote the introductory text for Part One, "An American Album," is a Photographic Archivist for the Smithsonian Archives. She is author of the series *Guide to Photographic Collections at the Smithsonian*, its first volume published by the Smithsonian Press in 1989. Ms. Vogt O'Connor was the *Images* book project's primary resources advisor.

Edwards Park contributed "Silver Men and Platinum Women." "Ted" Park is a founding editor of *Smithsonian* magazine, and author of several books including *Treasures of the Smithsonian*, published by Smithsonian Books. He currently writes on a variety of subjects, and his popular column, "Around the Mall and Beyond," appears regularly in *Smithsonian* magazine.

Robert Post wrote both text and captions for "Turning the Century." He is the editor of *Technology and Culture*, a journal publication of the Department of the History of Science and Technology at the Smithsonian's National Museum of American History. He has contributed to several Smithsonian Books publications, including *The American Land*, *The Smithsonian Book of Invention*, and *Every Four Years*.

William F. Stapp, who wrote "America Seeks Its Destiny," has served as Curator of Photographs at the Smithsonian's National Portrait Gallery since 1976. A historian, he specializes in the earliest years of photography. He co-authored *Picture It!* and was the primary author of *Robert Cornelius: Portraits from the Dawn of Photography* and has published numerous articles. William Stapp was also an overall *Images* project advisor.

John Thompson, author of the captions for "The Promised Land," lives in Washington D.C. His writing credits include *The Washington Post* and National Geographic Society publications. He also writes fiction and poetry.

Gerry Van der Heuvel, who wrote "Lincoln—A Singular Vision," is a freelance writer living in the Washington D.C. area. She is the author of *Crowns of Thorns and Glory*, a biography of Mary Todd Lincoln and Varina Howell Davis, published by E.P. Dutton in 1988.

Jim Wallace, author of "Keep the Feeling Alive," is Director of the Office Printing and Photographic Services at the Smithsonian Institution. As a freelance news photographer in the 1960s, he covered civil rights demonstrations in North Carolina for UPI. He recently edited and designed *Reflections On The Wall*, The Vietnam Veteran's Memorial.

Wilcomb E. Washburn, author of "Moving On West," served as Curator of Political History at the National Museum of History and Technology, and President of the American Studies Association. He is Director of the Smithsonian's Office of American Studies, and was the project editor of *The History of Indian-White Relations* (part of the *Handbook of North American Indians* series) published by the Smithsonian Press in 1989.

ACKNOWLEDGMENTS

With Special Thanks:

A small group of Smithsonian staff people and associates from other institutions provided very valuable assistance at the earliest concept and planning phases of this book. As noted, several authors were advisors as well.

Eugene Ostroff, Curator Supervisor, Division of Photographic History, NMAH; Sandra A. Babbidge, Museum Technician, Division of Photographic History, NMAH; Mary Grassick, Museum Technician, Division of Photographic History, NMAH; Herbert R. Collins, Executive Director, National Philatelic Collection, NMAH; Pete Daniel, Curator Supervisor, Division of Agriculture and National Resources, NMAH; Merry A. Foresta, Associate Curator, Department of Graphic Arts, NMAA; Sarah Greenough, Research Curator, NGA; David E. Haberstich, Archivist, Archives Center, NMAH; Peter Liebhold, Museum Technician, Division of Engineering and Industry, NMAH; Phyllis Rosenzweig, Associate Curator, Department of Painting and Sculpture, HMSG; Nancy Strader, former Smithsonian Books staff person, as of 1988 Director of the Corporate Photographic Archives for Digital Equipment Corporation, Maynard, Massachusetts; William Worthington, Jr., Museum Specialist, Division of Engineering and Industry, NMAH.

Acknowledgments
Richard Ahlborn, Curator, Division of Community Life, NMAH; David Black, Photo Services, CHM; Judy Chelnick, Museum Specialist, Division of Medical Sciences, NMAH; Diane Cook, Photo Order Clerk, NPG; Margaret Cooley, Museum Technician, Office of Photography, NGA; Deirdre Cross, Secretary, Division of Community Life, NMAH; B.J. Davis, Museum Specialist, Division of Musical Instruments, NMAH; Annie Dean, Museum Technician, Prints and Drawings, CHM; Elaine Evans Dee, Curator, Prints and Drawings, CHM; Nanci Edwards, Museum Specialist, Division of Agriculture and Natural Resources, NMAH; Peggy Feerick, Archives Specialist, Photographs, AAA; John Fleckner, Archivist, Archives Center, NMAH; Paula Fleming, Museum Specialist, National Anthropological Archives, NMNH; Shelly Foote, Museum Specialist, Division of Costume, NMAH; Juan Hamilton, Abiquiu, New Mexico; Margaret Harman, Photo Archivist, Juley Collection, NMAA; Michael Harris, Museum Specialist, Division of Medical Sciences, NMAH; Debra Hashim, Museum Specialist, Division of Armed Forces History, NMAH; Colleen Hennessey, Archivist, Freer Gallery of Art; Mary Humphreys, Volunteer, CHM; James Hutchins, Division of Armed Forces History, NMAH; Melissa Keiser, Museum Technician, Information Management, NASM; Claire Kelly, Assistant Curator of Exhibitions, NPG; Donald Kloster, Curator, Division of Armed Forces History, NMAH; Dr. Harold Langley, Curator, Division of Armed Forces History, NMAH; Arthur Lindo, Public Information Officer, CHM; Jennifer Locke, Museum Specialist, Division of Armed Forces History, NMAH; Mary Ellen McCaffrey, Production Control Officer, OPPS; Veronica McNiff, Public Information Assistant, CHM; Jane Morley, Fellow, Division of Engineering and Industry, NMAH; Alixa Naff, Archives Center, NMAH; Carlotta J. Owens, Assistant Curator, Prints and Drawings, NGA; Nancy Pope, Museum Technician/Librarian, National Philatelic Collection, NMAH; Jacqueline Rea, Volunteer, CHM; Mary Jean Fansler Rice, Eatontown, New Jersey; Harry Rubenstein, Museum Specialist, Division of Political History, NMAH; G. Terry Sharrer, Curator, Division of Agriculture and Natural Resources, NMAH; Abigail Terrones, Collections Manager, Department of Graphic Arts, NMAA; Stephen Van Dyk, Chief Librarian, CHM; Lois Vann, Museum Specialist, Division of Textiles, NMAH; Pearline Waldrop, Secretary, Exhibits Department, AMU; Jacqueline Washington, Library Technician, Central Reference Services, NMNH; John White Jr., Curator, Division of Transportation, NMAH; Roger White, Museum Specialist, Division of Transportation, NMAH.

Suppliers and Organizations
Charles Atkinson, Lehigh Press Lithographers; David Bartlett, Tom Suzuki, Inc.; Jerry Benitez, Stanford Paper; Dick Blackburn, York Graphic Services, Inc.; Jack Colahan, York Graphic Services, Inc.; Timothy Cook, Tom Suzuki, Inc.; Ansia Dial, Colorfax Photographic Labs, Inc.; Constance Dillman, Tom Suzuki, Inc.; Ronald Harlowe, Harlowe Typographers, Inc.; Bob Jillson, Holliston; Pete Jurgaitis, Lehigh Press Lithographers; John King, R.R. Donnelley & Sons Company; Library of Congress, Prints & Photographs Division; Bill Meals, York Graphic Services, Inc.; Cliff Mears, R.R. Donnelley & Sons Company; Treng Teng Mc Morrow, Tom Suzuki, Inc.; National Archives, Still Picture Branch; Steve Smith, Harlowe Typographers, Inc.; Nancy Strait, Tom Suzuki, Inc.; Virginia Suzuki, Tom Suzuki, Inc.; Joseph Vicino, Harlowe Typographers, Inc.; Ed Watters, The Lehigh Press, Inc.

PICTURE CREDITS

Abbreviations are used to identify Smithsonian Institution collections and other sources.

Smithsonian Institution (SI)

AAA	Archives of American Art
AMU	Anacostia Museum
CHM	Cooper-Hewitt Museum
HMSG	Hirshhorn Museum & Sculpture Garden
NASM	National Air and Space Museum
NMAA	National Museum of American Art
NMAH	National Museum of American History
	AC Archives Center
	AFH Division of Armed Forces History
	ANR Division of Agriculture and Natural Resources
	DC Division of Costume
	DT Division of Transportation
	EI Division of Engineering and Industry
	EMP Division of Electricity and Modern Physics
	MI Division of Musical Instruments
	MS Division of Medical Sciences
	NPC National Philatelic Collection
	PHH Division of Photographic History
	PLH Division of Political History
NMNH	National Museum of Natural History
NAA	National Anthropological Archives
NPG	National Portrait Gallery
OPPS	Office of Printing & Photographic Services

Other Sources

LC	Library of Congress
NA	National Archives
NGA	National Gallery of Art

Credits include picture negative numbers and photographer names when known. The negative numbers will assist anyone who wishes to obtain a print of any *Images* photograph in the public domain. Many of the sources are in Washington D.C., and, with the negative number that accompanies the particular credit, photos can be ordered. Correspondence or a preliminary call directly to the photo source is recommended.

Legend: L Left; R Right; T Top; C Center; B Bottom.

Jacket Front H.R. Buser, NMAH/PHH (86-9720); *Back* Gertrude Käsebier, NMAH/PHH (86-2205); *Flap* NMAH/AC (86-12835) Naff Arab-American Collection.

Front Matter p. 1 Rudolf Eickemeyer, Jr., NMAH/PHH (86-11389); 2-3 LC (LC-USZ62-38628); 4-5 Carnegie Library of Pittsburgh (A-176); 6 Alexander Gardner, NPG (NPG.81.M1); 8-9 Eadweard Muybridge, NMAH/PHH (89-7713); 11 Arnold Genthe, LC.

Part 1 An American Album pp. 12-13 Rudolf Eickemeyer, Jr., NMAH/PHH (79-11060); 14-15 NMAH/PHH (83-13176).

Silver Men and Platinum Women p. 16 Henry Fitz, Jr., NMAH/PHH (44-215A); 17 NPG (NPG.80.248); 18T Collection R. Bruce Duncan, copy photo Pat Lanza; 18B American Philosophical Library (675); 19 LC (LC-USZ62-10986); 20 NMAH/PHH (87-4587); 21T Mathew Brady Studio, NPG (NPG.85.78); 21B NMAH/PHH (86-10045); 22 Mathew Brady Studio, NMAH/PHH (86-12308); 23 Titian Peale, NMAH/PHH (84-2927); 24-25 David F. Barry, NMNH/NAA (3189-B-9); 25T NMAH/DT (42675-A); 25B NMNH/NAA (6394); 26T Rudolf Eickemeyer, Jr., NMAH/PHH (86-11374); 26B Hillel Burger, Peabody Museum, Harvard University (N27432); 26-27 Rudolf Eickemeyer, Jr., NMAH/PHH (85-1489); 28T Mark Twain Papers, The Bancroft Library, University

of California, Berkeley; 28B Courtesy Alexander Graham Bell Association for the Deaf; 28-29 Isabel V. Lyon, NPG (NPG.79.164); 30 LC (LC-USZ62-55131); 31L AAA, The Elihu Vedder Papers, copy photo Pat Lanza; 31R Thomas Eakins, HMSG (83.119), transferred from HMSG Archives, 1983; 32T G.P.A. Healy(?), AAA, The Marie de Mare Papers, copy photo Pat Lanza; 32B Thomas Eakins, HMSG (83.105), transferred from HMSG Archives, 1983; 32-33 AAA, Artists in their Paris Studios Collection, copy photo Pat Lanza; 34-35 Eadweard Muybridge, NPG (NPG.84.134); 36-37 NMAH/EI (88-9504); 37T International Museum of Photography at George Eastman House (1318); 37B Courtesy John F. Ross, copy photo Mark Gulezian; 38 Rudolf Eickemeyer, Jr., NMAH/PHH (86-11370); 39L NPG (NPG.84.127); 39R Nickolas Muray, NPG (T/NPG.78.151), permission by Mimi Muray; 40-41 Wilbur Sandison, Whatcom Museum of History and Art, Bellingham, WA; 41R Nickolas Muray, NPG (T/NPG.78.190.87), permission by Mimi Muray.

How We Like to See Ourselves p. 42 (detail) Pach Brothers Studio, NPG (NPG.77.134); 43 International Museum of Photography at George Eastman House (5253); 44L Courtesy Barbara B. Johnston, copy photo Mark Gulezian; 44-45 Courtesy Annie Waller, copy photo Mark Gulezian; 46-47 John Swartz(?), NPG (NPG.82.66), gift of Pinkerton's, Inc.; 47T NPG (NPG.81.138); 47B NPG (NPG.88.206); 48L Rudolf Eickemeyer, Jr., NMAH/PHH (86-11365); 48-49 NMAH/PHH (81-7434); 50 NMAH/PHH (86-11519); 51T NMAH/PHH (89-7711), copy photo Pat Lanza; 51B NMAH/PHH (86-11525); 52-53 LC (LC-USZ62-58272); 53T NMAH/PHH (83-223); 53B NMAH/PHH (81-4234); 54-55 LC (LC-USZ62-58968); 55T LC (LC-USZ62-47339); 55B NMAH/EI (85-133); 56-57 NMAH/DT (89-7710), copy photo Pat Lanza.

Part 2 America Seeks Its Destiny pp. 58-59 Thomas Eakins, NPG (NPG.79.69); 60-61 Mathew Brady, NA (111-B-446).

Lincoln—A Singular Vision p. 62 Mathew Brady, LC (LC-USP6-2416-A); 63 NPG (Graphics File); 64 LC (LC-B811-2300); 65 Cook Collection, Valentine Museum, Richmond, VA (CC1449); 66-67 Mathew Brady, NA (111-B-438); 67T H.B. Hull(?), NPG (NPG.77.57); 67B NA (111-B-3368); 68 NA (111-B-82); 69T LC (LC-B8184-B526); 69B Mathew Brady, NA (111-B-314); 70T NMAH/AFH (89-7702), copy photo Pat Lanza; 70B NMAH/AFH (41686); 71 NMAH/PHH (84-9312); 72-73 Mathew Brady, NA (111-B-223); 73T NMAH/PHH (81-9305); 73B LC (LC-B8161-7934); 74T LC (LC-B815-428); 74B Alexander Gardner, NPG (NPG.80.106); 74-75 Mathew Brady, LC (LC-B8171-671); 76-77 NA (111-B-349); 77T LC (LC-B8171-7046); 77B NMAH/PLH (74-3392); 78-79 LC (LC-B8184-8499); 78B NA (111-BA-1459); 79B NA (111-B-4762); 80-81 NA (111-BA-1395); 81T LC (LC-B8171-4016); 81B NA (111-B-3351); 82-83 NA (111-B-357); 83T NA (111-B-4975); 83B NA (111-B-4975A); 84 Alexander Gardner, LC (LC-B8171-7773); 85T LC (LC-USZ62-11964); 85B Mathew Brady, LC (LC-B8184-10701); 86-87 NA (111-B-137).

Moving on West p. 88 William Henry Jackson, Colorado Historical Society (F-24,094); 89 LC (LC-USZ62-1391); 90-91 William Shew, NMAH/PHH (38416C, 38416D, 38416E); 91T New Bedford Whaling Museum (3780); 92-93 Carleton E. Watkins, CHM (1976-23-15), anonymous gift, copy photo John Parnell/Art Resource, NY; 93T Carleton E. Watkins, CHM (1976-23-28), anonymous gift, copy photo John Parnell/Art Resource, NY; 93B Carleton E. Watkins, The Beinecke Rare Book and Manuscript Library, Yale University (88-973-M); 94T J.E. Whitney, LC (LC-USZ62-11024); 94B Courtesy A.J. Russell Union Pacific Museum (H1-21); 95 LC, courtesy AMU; 96T W.H. Illingworth, NA (77-HQ-264-854); 96B NMAH/AFH (89-7706), copy photo Pat Lanza; 97T O.S. Goff, Denver Public Library, Western History Department (07954); 97B W.H. Illingworth, LC (LC-USZ62-47876); 98-99 John C.H. Grabill, LC

(LC-USZ62-19725); 99R Gertrude Käsebier, NMAH/PHH (86-2205); 100-101 NMNH/NAA (55515); 101T NMNH/NAA (55514); 101B The Bettmann Archive (W350); 102-103 NMAH/NPC (88-19891); 103T LC (LC-USZ62-2132); 104T Rudolf Eickemeyer, Jr., NMAH/PHH (86-11382); 104B LC (LC-USZ62-68211); 105 David F. Barry, Denver Public Library, Western History Department (08027); 106-107 NMNH/NAA (44356); 107R NA (111-SC-85759).

Turning the Century p. 108 George Barker, LC (LC-USZ62-7418); 109 NMAH/EI (89-7667), copy photo Pat Lanza; 110B Courtesy Caterpillar, Inc.; 110-111 NMAH/ANR (61645-B); 112 NMAH/EI (48618); 113T NMAH/EI (89-7670), copy photo Pat Lanza; 113B NMAH/EI (89-7669), copy photo Pat Lanza; 114L NMAH/EI (89-7668), copy photo Pat Lanza; 114-115 NMAH/EI (86-894); 116-117T NMAH/PHH (72-10645); 116-117B NMAH/PHH (89-7712), copy photo Pat Lanza; 118T LC (LC-USZ62-12981); 118B NMAH/DT (74085); 118-119 LC (LC-USZ62-25403); 120-121 NMAH/DT (19886-B); 121T NASM (4485-C); 121B LC (LC-USZ62-55457); 122T LC (LC-USZ62-89688); 122B NMAH/EI (83-3180); 123 NMAH/EI (85-131); 124 Huestis P. Cook, Cook Collection, Valentine Museum, Richmond, VA (1030); 125T Courtesy AT&T Archives (HB-312); 125B NMAH/EMP; 126-127 NMAH/PLH (72-6484); 127R NMAH/PLH (72-6483); 128-129 1. Courtesy The Gillette Company, 2. Courtesy Hershey Foods Corporation, 3. Courtesy The Coca-Cola Company, 4. American Red Cross (A14533A), 5. Courtesy Kraft Archives, 6. Courtesy H.J. Heinz Company, 7. Courtesy Milton Bradley Company, A Subsidiary of Hasbro, Inc., 8. Courtesy I. Magnin, 9. & 10. Courtesy Sears Archives, 11. Courtesy Stetson Hat Company, 12. Courtesy Levi Strauss and Company, 13. Courtesy Parker Pen USA Ltd.; 130-131 Courtesy The Senate Historical Office; 132-133 NMAH/AFH (89-7705), copy photo Pat Lanza; 133T John C.H. Grabill, LC (LC-USZ62-17591); 133B

NMAH/AFH (89-7704), copy photo Pat Lanza; 134T NASM/Department of Aeronautics; 134B NASM (85-8305); 135 NASM (A-4133); 136-137 NMAH/AFH (89-7703), copy photo Pat Lanza; 137R NPG (NPG.78.161).

Part 3 America—A Family Affair pp. 138-139 Rudolf Eickemeyer, Jr., NMAH/PHH (77-7001); 140B NMAH/PHH (81-9310); 140-141T LC (LC-USZ62-57156); 140-141B LC.

The Promised Land p. 142 NMAH/AC (86-10460) Carlos de Wendler-Funaro Gypsy Research Collection; 143 NMAH/AC (86-12826) Naff Arab-American Collection; 144-145 Lewis W. Hine, AAA, The Elizabeth McCausland Papers, copy photo Pat Lanza; 146 Edwin Levick, NMAH/DC (73-11583); 147T LC (LC-USZ62-22339); 147B, 148T, & 148B Lewis W. Hine, AAA, The Elizabeth McCausland Papers, copy photo Pat Lanza; 148-149 NMAH/DT (32-602-B); 150-151 NMNH/NAA (89-1584); 151R Courtesy Tom Suzuki, copy photo Mark Gulezian; 152L Terry Evans, NMAA (1983.63.1807), transfer from National Endowment for the Arts; 152-153 Seaver Center for Western History Research, Natural History Museum of Los Angeles County (4670); 154-155 James Mooney, NMNH/NAA (1044-B); 155R NMNH/NAA (56,767); 156-157 James Mooney, NMNH/NAA (1824-D).

Little Ol' New York et al p. 158 U.S. Department of Commerce, NOAA-NOS Photogrammetry Branch; 159 Lewis W. Hine, AAA, The Elizabeth McCausland Papers, copy photo Pat Lanza; 160-161 Museum of the City of New York; 161T George Collins Cox, NMAH/PHH (81-10252); 162-163 Courtesy AT&T Archives (H-1849-0); 163T Alfred Stieglitz, NGA (1949.3.73) Alfred Stieglitz Collection; 163C Courtesy AT&T Archives (HB-1387-6); 163B Berenice Abbott, NMAH/PHH (85-15302); 164-165 NMAH/MS (79-12777); 165T Berenice Abbott, NMAH/PHH (85-15296); 165B Lewis W. Hine, NMAH/PHH (74-5809); 166T Lewis W. Hine, AAA, The Elizabeth McCausland Papers, copy photo Pat Lanza; 166B NMAH/MS (79-12772); 166-167 NMAH/MS (79-12769); 168 LC (LC-USZ62-80310); 169T Frances Benjamin Johnston, AAA, The Charles Caffin Papers, copy photo Pat Lanza; 169B LC (LC-USZ62-72014); 170 CHM/CHM Archives, copy photo John Parnell/Art Resource, NY; 171 NMAH/PHH (83-4644); 172-173 Berenice Abbott, NMAA (1975.83.15), transfer from General Services Administration through Evander Childs High School; 173TL NMAH/EI (89-7662), copy photo Pat Lanza; 173TR NMAH/EI (89-7661), copy photo Pat Lanza; 173C NMAH/NPC (74514); 173B LC (LC-USZ62-056928); 174 Alfred Stieglitz, NGA (1980.70.49) Alfred Stieglitz Collection; 175TL Alfred Stieglitz, NGA (1980.70.7) Alfred Stieglitz Collection; 175TR Alfred Stieglitz, NGA (1949.3.303) Alfred Stieglitz Collection; 175B Alfred Stieglitz, NGA (1949.3.1188) Alfred Stieglitz Collection; 176T from Martin Williams, *Jazz Masters of New Orleans*, 1967, The Macmillan Company, NY, copy photo Pat Lanza; 176B NMAH/AC (89-7681) Duke Ellington Collection, copy photo Pat Lanza; 177 NMAH/MI (89-7698), copy photo Mark Gulezian; 178 NMAH/DC (89-7699), copy photo Pat Lanza; 179T NMAH/DC (89-7700), copy photo Pat Lanza; 179B Rudolf Eickemeyer, Jr., NMAH/PHH (81-4237); 180-181 LC (LC-USA7-5044); 181T NA (111-BA-1444); 181B NMAH/EI (85-17489); 182-183 NMAH/DT (48479); 183R LC (LC-USZ62-21831).

At Home in the Hinterlands p. 184 NMAH/PHH (84-1613); 185 NMAH/AC (89-7682) Naff Arab-American Collection, copy photo Pat Lanza; 186-187 NMAH/PLH (85-16967); 187T LC (LC-USZ62-36829); 188-189 NMAH/ANR (84-8593); 189T Rudolf Eickemeyer, Jr., NMAH/PHH (87-3129); 189B NMAH/EI (89-7671), copy photo Pat Lanza; 190-191 Marine Biological Laboratory, Woods Hole, MA; 191T Lewis W. Hine, AAA, The Elizabeth McCausland Papers, copy photo Pat Lanza; 191B NMAH/ARN

(89-7689), copy photo Pat Lanza; 192T NMAH/NPC (86-4987); 192B NMAH/NPC (86-921); 192-193 G.W. Ackerman, NA (33-FRA-S-15754C); 194T NMAH/ANR (79-2514); 194B LC (LC-USZ62-19632); 194-195 NMAH/ANR (67319); 196-197 NMAH/ANR (86-3488); 197T NMAH/ANR (86-3509); 197B LC; 198T LC (LC-USZ62-45990); 198B NA (16-G-121-1-2); 198-199 LC (LC-USZ62-16565); 200-201 Marion Post Wolcott, LC (LC-USF34-52628-D); 201T NMAH/ANR (85-18164); 201B NMAH/ANR (89-7690), copy photo Pat Lanza; 202T Russell Lee, LC (LC-USF-3301-12327); 202B Dorothea Lange, LC (LC-USF34-19911-E); 202-203 LC (LC-USF34-40841); 204T NMAH/ANR (89-7695), copy photo Mark Gulezian; 204B NMAH/ANR (89-7691), copy photo Pat Lanza; 204-205 NMAH/ANR (89-7693), copy photo Pat Lanza; 206 LC (LC-USF34-62097); 207T LC (LC-USZ62-88923); 207B Rudolf Eickemeyer, Jr., NMAH/PHH (83-8199); 208T NMAH/PLH (75102); 208B NMAH/PLH (75101); 208-209 NA (111-SC-101620); 210-211 LC (LC-USZ62-64114).

Part 4 Taking Our Show on the Road pp. 212-213 NMAH/AFH (89-7701), copy photo Pat Lanza; 214-215 NASM (88-18661).

Twentieth Century Unlimited p. 216 NMAH/DT (89-7709), copy photo Pat Lanza; 217 NMAH/DT (89-5674); 218-219 NMAH/DT (78-3565); 219T NA (111-SC-11887); 219B NMAH/EI (89-7663), copy photo Pat Lanza; 220T NA (111-SC-12151); 220B NMAH/AFH (77-12276); 220-221 NMAH/AFH (88-16825); 222-223 LC (LC-USZ62-45005); 223R NASM (75-7024); 224T NMAH/EI (89-7664), copy photo Pat Lanza; 224B NMAH/EI (89-7665), copy photo Pat Lanza; 224-225 NASM (84-9563); 226T LC (LC-USZ62-60681); 226B NMAH/AC (83-16783) George H. Clark Radioana Collection; 227 NMAH/AC (89-7679) George H. Clark Radioana Collection, copy photo Pat Lanza; 228-229 1. Doris Ulmann, NPG (NPG.78.2), permission by University of Oregon Li-

brary, 2. Nickolas Muray, NPG (T/NPG.78.192.93), permission by Mimi Muray, 3. Nickolas Muray, NPG (NPG.78.8), permission by Mimi Muray, 4. Carl Van Vechten, NPG (NPG.76.86), permission by Estate of Carl Van Vechten, Joseph Solomon, Executor, 5. Clara E. Sipprell, NPG (NPG.82.181), 6. Berenice Abbott, NPG (NPG.76.83), permission by Commerce Graphics Ltd., Inc., 7. Man Ray, NPG (NPG.81.141), © ARS NY/ADAGP, 1989, 8. Wide World Photos, NPG (NPG.82.TC95), gift of Time, Inc.; 230T NMAH/MS; 230B Courtesy The Kellogg Company; 231 LC (LC-USZ62-80256); 232-233 NMAH/ANR (89-7686), copy photo Pat Lanza; 233T NA (80-G-16871); 233C Russell C. Aikens, NMAH/ANR (89-7688), copy photo Pat Lanza; 233B Russell C. Aikens, NMAH/ANR (89-7687), copy photo Pat Lanza; 234-235 NA (210-G10-C839); 235T & 235BR National Japanese American Historical Society; 235BL Dorothea Lange, NA (210-G-2-C160); 236-237 LC (LC-USZ62-45642); 237T NASM (22130-AC) U.S. Air Force Photo Collection; 237B NMAH/ANR (89-7692), copy photo Pat Lanza; 238T NMAH/MS (83-15559); 238B NMAH/MS (84-354); 238-239 NMAH/MS (83-15553); 240-241 Courtesy The Senate Historical Office; 241R NASM (87299-AC) U.S. Air Force Photo Collection.

Keep the Feeling Alive p. 242 Mathew Brady, NMAH/PHH (72-2732); 243 NMAH/DC (76-7189); 244TL Thomas Eakins, Philadelphia Museum of Art (68-203-2), given by Seymour Adelman; 244BL NMAH/PHH (84-9303); 244BR NMAH/PHH (84-11985); 244-245 NMAH/PLH (31272); 245TL Courtesy Howard D. Rees, Frostburg, MD, copy photo Mark Gulezian; 245TR Courtesy Col. James S. Corbitt, Martin, TN, copy photo Mark Gulezian; 245BL Courtesy John Ware, Tucson, AZ, copy photo Mark Gulezian; 245BR NMAH/AFH, copy photo Mark Gulezian; 246TL NMAH/PHH (86-4499); 246TR Jeff Tinsley, OPPS (87-4914/19); 246BL NMAH/DT (79-1651); 247L OPPS; 247R Richard Hofmeister, OPPS.

INDEX

Two indexes follow: a subject listing keyed to the images themselves; and an index of major photographers whose work appears in the book. Please note that, where known, photographers are also listed in the photo credits.

SUBJECTS

The book's elegant design was created by
Tom Suzuki of Falls Church, Virginia.
Inspired by "Camera Work," a photoart
magazine published from 1903-1917 by
Alfred Steiglitz, Tom Suzuki also originated
exclusively for this edition a new display
type, *Images*, developing it on the Macintosh
with the Fontographer program. The text
type is eleven point Stempel Garamond
with captions ten point Stempel Garamond,
typeset by Harlowe Typography, Inc.,
Brentwood, Maryland. Heads and initial
capitals imageset by Unicorn Graphics,
Washington, D.C. Picture separation and
film preparation were provided by York
Graphic Services, Inc., of York, Pennsylvania, using primarily the DuPont
Highlight™ Monochrome Image Editing
System. The book was printed in Willard,
Ohio, by the R.R. Donnelley & Sons Company on Warrenflo Web Gloss with Eco-
logical Fibers Rainbow Antique endsheets,
bound in Holliston Payko with jacket
printing by Lehigh Press Lithographers,
Pennsauken, New Jersey.